# Quiz Therapy

*i*Village
Solutions™

# Quiz Therapy

## Eileen Livers, Editor

Rutledge Hill Press™
*Nashville, Tennessee*

A Division of Thomas Nelson, Inc.
*www.ThomasNelson.com*

Published by Rutledge Hill Press, a division of Thomas
Nelson, Inc., P.O. Box 141000, Nashville, Tennessee 37214.

**Library of Congress Cataloging-in-Publication Data**

Quiz therapy / Eileen Livers, editor.
      p. cm. — (iVillage solutions)
    ISBN 1-4016-0044-1 (pbk.)
    1. Women—Psychology—Miscellanea. 2. Man-
woman relationships—Miscellanea. I. Livers, Eileen.
II. Series.
   HQ1206.Q563 2003
   305.4—dc21                 2003000339

Printed in the United States of America

03 04 05 06 07 — 5 4 3 2 1

# Contents

## Chapter 3: Improve Your Dating Life

*And make the most of your Saturday nights*

## Chapter 4: Understand Your Man

*And find out if he's right for you*

## Chapter 5: Check Your Couple Compatibility

*And find out if your love will last*

The title at the top of the page reads:

## Chapter 10: Find Your Celebrity Match                      223

*And shine a spotlight on your inner star*

# Foreword

I'm a self-confessed quiz addict. When I was a teenager, I'd practically count down the days until my monthly magazine appeared in the mail. The first thing I'd flip to, pen in hand, was the quiz. As soon as I was done, I'd be on the phone to my girlfriends, comparing my score with theirs. My passion for quiz taking—and for sharing my results with my friends—continued on through college, during my early career years, and right on into the present. If there's a quiz to be taken, you can count me in, and all my friends know it—because I make them take them, too!

What is it about quizzes that I love so much? To me, they're like mini-therapy sessions. But in these therapy sessions you actually have fun. When you want to know why your love life is lacking *oomph,* if you're going to get that promotion at work, or which of your friends is really there for you, a quiz can provide valuable insight, plus give you an illuminating look at yourself—how your personality could be helping or hindering your love life, career, friendships, and more.

In this book, you'll find 55 revealing quizzes, covering every aspect of your life— from dating to sex to beauty. You don't have to read the book straight through; you can take the quizzes as you need them. And you may find yourself taking the same quiz more than once—things change. You can take all of these quizzes alone, but some are fun to do with friends—and in some cases, with family members or love mates. Then you can analyze your answers and compare scores. As a result, in the exciting process of discovering new things about yourself and getting to know yourself better, you'll get to know each other better, too. And have some fun!

# Contributors

Contributors to and consultants on the quizzes in this book include

Sherry Amatenstein

Karen Rauch Carter,
for "Do You Have Good or Bad Feng Shui?"

Gwynn Cassidy

Charity Curley

Leslie George

Nicole Gianuglou

Kate Hanley

Jennifer Hill

Regina Leeds,
for "Are You Addicted to Stuff?"

Beth Pratt

Lou Sagar,
for "What's Your Decorating Personality?"

Nina Sherwin

Agapi Stassinopoulos,
for "Which Goddess Are You?"

Amy Toffelmire

Jamie Turndorf, Ph.D.,
for "What's Your Fighting Style?"

# 1

# Discover the Inner You

**And find out how well you know yourself**

Which Goddess Are You?

How Happy Are You Really?

Will You Be Rich?

What Ice Cream Flavor Are You?

What Do Your Dreams Reveal about You?

# Which Goddess Are You?

The Greek goddesses have been inspiring women's self-awareness and touching their lives for thousands of years. How do the seven female divinities affect you? Take this test to find out which goddess you're ruled by—and learn how to awaken, restore, and reveal the natural powers of all of the goddesses within you.

**❶ What is the most important thing in your life?**

____ **a.** Marriage

____ **b.** Serving others

____ **c.** Romance and passion

____ **d.** Career

____ **e.** Independence

____ **f.** Finding myself

____ **g.** Children

**❷ What do you want most out of marriage?**

____ **a.** An equal partnership

____ **b.** The opportunity to create a warm, nurturing home life

____ **c.** Passion—without it, what is there?

____ **d.** Friendship—the key to a long-lasting relationship

____ **e.** You're not sure you will get married

____ **f.** A spiritual partnership

____ **g.** Children—you can't wait to be a mother

**❸ Your ideal life partner is**

____ **a.** Self-confident—someone who would never feel threatened by you

____ **b.** Service-oriented—someone who strives to do for others

____ **c.** Passionate—someone who is as loving and sexual as you are

____ **d.** Intelligent—someone with whom you can discuss all kinds of interesting topics

____ **e.** Independent—someone who believes partners can have their own lives

____ **f.** Mature and successful—someone whose position in the world is impressive

____ **g.** Stable and protective—someone who can provide for you and your family

**4** **When it comes to sex, you**

___ **a.** Enjoy the give and take that leads to mutual pleasure

___ **b.** Can take it or leave it—you feel fulfilled without it, as long as there is love in your relationship

___ **c.** Are easily aroused and thoroughly enjoy sex—with a desired partner, of course

___ **d.** Usually feel awkward and disconnected from your body—it's hard to let go of what's going in your head and let your body enjoy the experience

___ **e.** May seem aloof and withdrawn at first, but once you relax and get into it, anything can happen

___ **f.** Find it to be a powerful, almost transforming experience

___ **g.** Enjoy pleasing your partner but don't usually focus on having your own needs met

**5** **On a typical free Saturday afternoon, you would most likely be found**

___ **a.** Attending a meeting for your church or synagogue, or other local association

___ **b.** Gardening or doing housework

___ **c.** Shopping or visiting an art museum with friends, or getting a massage

___ **d.** Attending a lecture series or author reading, or curled up with a good book

___ **e.** Doing something athletic outdoors, such as hiking or sailing

___ **f.** Reading your horoscope, meditating, or participating in some other New Age practice

___ **g.** In the kitchen cooking and possibly preparing to entertain at home that evening

**6** **If you were to throw a luncheon for your friends, whose names would be on your guest list?**

___ **a.** The wives and girlfriends of your mate's friends

___ **b.** Women you've met while doing volunteer work in the community

___ **c.** A fun group of girlfriends you feel comfortable sharing *everything* with

___ **d.** Mostly men friends—you have more of them than female friends

___ **e.** A few very close, carefully chosen friends

___ **f.** A small group of friends with whom you share an almost spiritual connection

___ **g.** Women who have children the same age as yours

**7** A friend calls to invite you to a party next Saturday night. You

____ **a.** Attend and stay close to your partner—you two tend to mingle together

____ **b.** Find a way to get out of it—you'd rather spend the time at home

____ **c.** Can't wait to go—you love to be the life of the party

____ **d.** Go and participate in a group conversation about current events, politics, or work

____ **e.** Mingle freely, never spending too much time with any one person or group

____ **f.** Go and get involved in a heavy conversation with one person

____ **g.** Help the host or hostess in the kitchen and make sure everyone is having a good time

**8** Which profession most appeals to you?

____ **a.** Head of volunteer organization

____ **b.** Nurse or social worker

____ **c.** Clothing designer, actress/singer, or public relations person

____ **d.** Lawyer or business executive

____ **e.** Adventure guide or camp leader

____ **f.** Psychotherapist

____ **g.** Restaurant owner or chef/caterer

**9** If you could create your dream home anywhere, where would it be?

____ **a.** Beverly Hills, California, or a similarly elegant neighborhood

____ **b.** In a gated community—you want the protection and privacy

____ **c.** In a deluxe apartment building filled with gold tones and rich colors and fabrics

____ **d.** In New York City or another fast-paced, stimulating city

____ **e.** In the country, near parks and other open spaces

____ **f.** Doesn't matter, as long as it has a calm and peaceful energy

____ **g.** In a tight-knit community, where neighbors feel comfortable dropping by for a cup of coffee

**10** When you have free time, how do you like to spend it?

____ **a.** Socializing with friends or attending a social event

____ **b.** Doing volunteer work

____ **c.** Shopping, especially for clothes

____ **d.** Going to a bookstore or spending time reading

____ **e.** Taking a walk outdoors

____ **f.** Meditating or otherwise spending some quiet time alone with your thoughts

____ **g.** Cooking for family and friends

**⓫ Your clothing closet is filled mostly with**

____ **a.** Simple, classic styles that allow you to look put-together but not fussy or trendy

____ **b.** A hodgepodge of items purchased without much thought or planning

____ **c.** Clothes that mold to your body in soft, luxurious fabrics

____ **d.** Outfits you feel confident in and know will make a positive impression

____ **e.** Exercise clothing, jeans, and other comfortable, casual clothes

____ **f.** Artsy, somewhat eccentric items

____ **g.** Simple, comfortable items that are good for lounging in at home and playing with children

**⓬ Which of the following statements is most true for you?**

____ **a.** You like your body best when you know that your partner finds you attractive.

____ **b.** Your outward appearance matters less to you than how you feel on the inside.

____ **c.** Your body makes you feel sexy and attractive.

____ **d.** You don't spend much time thinking about your body.

____ **e.** You take care of your body so that you can exercise and be active.

____ **f.** You are struggling to make peace with your body.

____ **g.** What you like best about your body is its ability to bear children.

## Scoring

Add up the number of As, Bs, Cs, Ds, Es, Fs, and Gs you chose. If you chose one letter more than any of the others, that represents the goddess who rules your personality the most. If you have the same number of more than one letter, several goddesses influence your personality evenly. Also note the goddesses who influence you to a lesser degree. Every woman has aspects of *all* seven goddesses in her personality. To achieve a healthy balance, you need to integrate characteristics of each into your life. Now that you have identified the qualities of the goddesses in yourself, you can recognize needs you have left unfulfilled. And by attending to those needs, you can become happier and more self-confident.

(Mostly As)
### Hera

If you possess many of Hera's qualities, you tend to find fulfillment in relationships and look on marriage as permanent.

In marriage you feel no sense of frustration or resentment, because you are an equal partner with your spouse. You are confident and have no trouble asserting your authority in and out of the relationship. You seek men who are self-confident and successful, because you are comfortable with the concept that you can be fulfilled through him (and he through you). As long as your partner honors the marriage as much as you do and appreciates you, you will be happy. If he doesn't, you must concentrate on your own growth and discover an identity independent of him. To do that, add more of the goddess Artemis to your life.

(Mostly Bs)
## Hestia

If you embody the qualities of Hestia, you understand the value of having your own sacred place, whether it's an actual room or simply a time of day when you free your mind of busy thoughts and experience peace of mind. This place is in your home—where you feel the most joy. You are at home with yourself, however, wherever you are and no matter whom you are with. You know that the meaning of your life springs from your spiritual center. This brings you a great sense of security. You do not crave attention or material possessions; you nurture your friends and family with your unconditional love.

(Mostly Cs)
## Aphrodite

If you are ruled mostly by Aphrodite, your femininity and passionate spirit are the controlling forces in your life. You tend to be charismatic and self-assured, comfortable with your body, and unrestrained sexually. Men are drawn to you like bees to flowers, which satisfies your erotic nature. However, you tend not to form permanent attachments with lovers because you value your sexual freedom, which may leave you feeling lonely and even depleted once a relationship ends. To find and form a more lasting relationship, add more of the goddess Hera to your life.

(Mostly Ds)
## Athena

If Athena rules you, you are bright-eyed, shrewd, resourceful, and inventive. With friends, you are the wise counselor—always ready with an empowering message. You believe strongly that women can accomplish anything men can: No wonder you put so much time into your career. Athena women tend to be ruled by their head, not their heart. You carefully guard your intimate side, protecting your emotions and vulnerability. To awaken your unexpressed womanliness, use the passion you apply to your intellectual achievements. Work to integrate your strong masculine side with your feminine side—bringing together your strength with your vulnerability, your creativity with caring, and your intelligence with imagination. (Take lessons from the goddesses Hestia and Aphrodite.) Otherwise, you risk coming off as unaffectionate and self-righteous.

(Mostly Es)
### Artemis

If Artemis rules you, your independent spirit belongs to no one but yourself. Your body is vibrant, your attitude robust, and your manner vigorous and alive. You are driven by physical rather than mental energy. You feel complete without a man in your life and would never compromise your essential nature for a romantic partner. You are skilled at establishing personal boundaries and enter into relationships on your own terms—in short, you can take care of yourself.

(Mostly Fs)
### Persephone

If you exemplify the qualities of Persephone, you have most likely experienced great loss in your life—the loss of your health or emotional or physical security, betrayal of a friend or lover, the loss of a child, or your own divorce or that of your parents. This has forced you to face your dark, unenlightened side (the side that blames other people or circumstances for your own suffering) and transform yourself into a stronger, more independent, more accepting, and more loving person. It may have also led you down a spiritual path, and moved you to place great emphasis on inner calm and on close connections with friends. Because you can embrace, integrate, and accept difficult experiences, you offer others the gift of empathy—you know where they are or have been. Don't forget to enjoy life's pleasures, calling forth the qualities of Aphrodite and Artemis that are within you.

(Mostly Gs)
### Demeter

If you fit the Demeter archetype, you are a nurturer and caretaker. You have a generous heart and enjoy extending your love to others. You are motivated by the most powerful of instincts—to give life—and you selflessly devote yourself to the life you create. You feel compelled to care for all those around you, even if they are not your own children. In short, you feel the need to be all things to all people and therefore your own needs sometimes go unmet. You must learn to say no, and apply Artemis's sense of boundaries and Aphrodite's ability to put herself first. That way, you can give to others from an overflowing rather than a half-full cup.

Source: *Conversations with the Goddesses: Revealing the Divine Power Within You*, by Agapi Stassinopoulos (Stewart, Tabori & Chang, 1999).

# How Happy Are You Really?

"Don't worry, be happy" is easier sung than lived. How contented are you? Answer these questions and find out if you're living a happy life—and what you can do to boost your bliss.

**1** In general, your life feels like
____ **a.** A mix of good and bad days
____ **b.** An exciting adventure
____ **c.** A struggle

**2** How satisfied are you with your friendships?
____ **a.** Very—you feel grateful to know the people that you do.
____ **b.** Somewhat—you have your good times, but often wish you were closer to your friends.
____ **c.** You're pretty disappointed—your friends just don't seem to understand you.

**3** When was the last time you ate your favorite food?
____ **a.** So long ago that you can hardly remember what your favorite food is
____ **b.** About one month ago
____ **c.** Very recently

**4** If someone took a snapshot of you at your desk, you would probably look
____ **a.** Somewhat stressed
____ **b.** Worn down and worn out
____ **c.** Busy but full of energy

**5** How would you feel if someone asked you to make a list of your accomplishments?
____ **a.** Surprised—you'd be flattered that someone was interested.
____ **b.** Pleased—you're proud of your accomplishments.
____ **c.** Insecure—you don't have much to list.

**6** Your personal mantra could be
____ **a.** "I'm so tired—I need sleep!"
____ **b.** "I need an extra day in the week to get everything done!"
____ **c.** "I'm ready for anything."

**7** How do you feel when you meet new people?

____ **a.** Relaxed—you like meeting new people and think that most people enjoy meeting you.

____ **b.** Nervous—you worry about making a good impression.

____ **c.** Somewhat shy—you need a few minutes to get comfortable.

**8** When faced with an obstacle, you

____ **a.** Feel certain that you will not reach your goal

____ **b.** Feel unsure about the chances of reaching your goal

____ **c.** Feel confident about reaching your goal

**9** The following sentence best describes the way you feel about your appearance:

____ **a.** You like the way you look.

____ **b.** You think you look okay.

____ **c.** You don't like the way you look.

**10** How would your friends or family describe you when you're doing your favorite activity?

____ **a.** Pleased, but you don't get to do it as often as you'd like.

____ **b.** Delighted and 100 percent focused.

____ **c.** Favorite activity? You don't have time for one!

**11** How do you feel about the place you are in your life right now?

____ **a.** You've accomplished a few goals but still have many more to go to fulfill your dreams.

____ **b.** You're nowhere near the place you wanted to be at this age.

____ **c.** You've done a lot and are pretty pleased with where you are.

**12** To you, laughing is something you

____ **a.** Enjoy regularly in your life

____ **b.** Enjoy but wish you could do more of

____ **c.** Really miss in your life

**13** When it comes to making major decisions, you usually

____ **a.** Beat yourself up, agonizing over your choices

____ **b.** Consider the pros and cons, then do your best to make the right choice

____ **c.** Go with your gut and never look back

**14** **Whenever you feel down about your life, your first thought is**

____ **a.** Life's not easy, but it'll pass.

____ **b.** Why me?

____ **c.** Everything will work out for the best—it always does.

# Scoring

Give yourself the numerical value that matches each of your answers. Then add all 14 scores together and use your total score to find your result category.

1. a – 2   b – 3   c – 1
2. a – 3   b – 2   c – 1
3. a – 1   b – 2   c – 3
4. a – 2   b – 1   c – 3
5. a – 2   b – 3   c – 1
6. a – 1   b – 2   c – 3
7. a – 3   b – 1   c – 2
8. a – 1   b – 2   c – 3
9. a – 3   b – 2   c – 1
10. a – 2   b – 3   c – 1
11. a – 2   b – 1   c – 3
12. a – 3   b – 2   c – 1
13. a – 1   b – 2   c – 3
14. a – 2   b – 1   c – 3

**(33–42 points)**

## On Cloud Nine

It's amazing. While the rest of the world is counting gray hairs—wondering what to be when they grow up or wishing the kids would nap or that the boss would stop sending them projects—you are accomplishing your dreams and reveling in your own beautiful life. From delicious food to laughter, you know what it takes to make yourself happy. Plus you have discovered how to connect in a meaningful and satisfying way with those around you. In short, you try your best to live each day to the fullest. The best part of your contented condition is that it's contagious. You seem so comfortable in your own skin that the people around you see you as a happy person and respond with love and respect.

**(23–32 points)**

## Off Course to Bliss

You haven't given much thought to your happiness in a long time, which explains why you're not sitting on top of the world. To be happy, you have to *know* what makes you happy and work to incorporate those things into your life. Lately you've just been going through the motions without questioning much of anything—your work, your friendships, how you spend your free time. There may be things in your life that *do* make you happy, but you need to focus on doing more of what you want to do and on having fun. You may be judging your-self and planning your life based on what other people think. If this sounds famil-iar, work to shake the habit of living your life this way. Pay more attention to what interests and pleases *you*, and you're sure to be charting a course to a happier life.

(14–22 points)
## Down but Not Out

Joy has not left you behind. But your harsh judgment of yourself and your pes-simistic view of your life are seriously hurting your chances of happiness. It may not be what life brings you that is making you unhappy—but the way you react to it. As Martha Washington once said, "The greater part of our happiness or misery depends on our dispositions and not on our circumstances." Even if you feel that your life is off course or down-right disappointing, you have the power to change things starting this minute.

What do you need to do to achieve happiness? Start by focusing more on what you have that's good in your life. You may be surprised by how full your half-empty cup really is. Then think hard about what else you need to be truly content. Once you realize your core values and needs, you will be able to include them in your life and find the satisfaction you deserve.

# Will You Be Rich?

You don't have to play Lotto or appear on a game show to have a fortune in your future. But you *do* need the right attitude. Grab your lucky pen and find out if prosperity is probable for you—and what you need to do to really strike it rich.

**1** **You hear through the grapevine about a new project at work that you would be perfect for. Do you say something to your boss?**

____ **a.** No—your boss knows how to dole out projects appropriately; if you're right for it, you'll get it.

____ **b.** Of course—how else will your boss know that you're interested?

____ **c.** Only if you have the time for the project—you want your boss to know you're available.

**2** **When it comes to school and grades (in the past or present), you would summarize your achievements as**

____ **a.** Top notch—you studied a lot and it usually paid off in good grades

____ **b.** Fair—you received average grades in return for your average efforts

____ **c.** Miserable—you were never lucky with grades

**3** **At your favorite coffee spot, you notice an extra chair next to a good-looking guy you would like to meet. You**

____ **a.** Walk by slowly and hope he asks you to join him

____ **b.** Are so nervous you just keep walking—really quickly!

____ **c.** Slide into the seat—what a break!

**4** **The people in your life who know your hopes and dreams are**

____ **a.** Your close friends

____ **b.** Your friends, your parents, even your classmates or coworkers

____ **c.** Your mother—and she knows only because she read your adolescent wishes in your high school diary

**5** There's a huge sale at your favorite store and your schedule is busy, busy, busy. You don't need any new clothes right now, but you do need a dress for a formal affair that's a few months away. You

____ **a.** Don't go to the sale—you're not in the mood for the sale scene, and there probably won't be anything left by the time you get there

____ **b.** Go to the sale but only for a limited time—you're not desperate for the dress, you're busy, and the sale is a mob scene

____ **c.** Make the time to go to the sale, and elbow your way through the crowds and the packed racks until you find your dream dress

**6** You get a call from a top headhunter who says there's a position open that you seem perfect for. You're happy in your current position. What do you do?

____ **a.** You speak with the headhunter on the phone—you don't mind taking a few minutes to hear about the opportunity and be nice to an influential recruiter.

____ **b.** You agree to set up a meeting with the headhunter—you always like to pursue opportunities.

____ **c.** You say thanks but no thanks—if you're happy where you are, what's the point of wasting anyone's time?

**7** At the mall, you notice a $1 raffle for the chance to win a new car. You

____ **a.** Buy a ticket—what have you got to lose?

____ **b.** Don't buy a ticket—it's impossible to win those things.

____ **c.** Buy a few tickets—you never know when it will be your lucky day.

**8** You've been promising yourself that you'll take a class to learn more about your favorite hobby. Two weeks before the semester starts, you

____ **a.** Are signed up for class

____ **b.** Have dog-eared your chosen class in the school catalog but have yet to register

____ **c.** Have yet to call to receive the school catalog

**9** When you are asked to step in as leader of your book club/volunteer organization/mother's group, you know it's because

____ **a.** No one else wants the job

____ **b.** Your devotion and efforts have paid off

____ **c.** It's your turn

# Scoring

Give yourself the numerical value that matches each of your answers. Then add all nine scores together and use your total score to find your result category.

1. **a** – 1  **b** – 3  **c** – 2
2. **a** – 3  **b** – 2  **c** – 1
3. **a** – 2  **b** – 1  **c** – 3
4. **a** – 2  **b** – 3  **c** – 1
5. **a** – 1  **b** – 2  **c** – 3
6. **a** – 2  **b** – 3  **c** – 1
7. **a** – 2  **b** – 1  **c** – 3
8. **a** – 3  **b** – 2  **c** – 1
9. **a** – 1  **b** – 3  **c** – 2

(21–27 points)

## Affluence Awaits You

No doubt success and prosperity will be part of your future. Don't be surprised if people who know you think your good fortune is all luck. They're right in a way, but what they don't realize is that you're working hard to create your own luck. How do you do it? You feel good about yourself and believe in your abilities, so you're not afraid to go after what you want. You have also mastered the art of putting yourself in the right places at the right time and taking advantage of all opportunities—self-generated and not. Your motto: Life is what you make it of it. And if it's a rich life you want, that's what you will receive—or rather, make for yourself!

(15–20 points)

## Riches Are within Reach

No one's knocking on your door with a multimillion-dollar check any time soon, but don't worry, you have the potential to live a prosperous life. Life is what you make of it: You can't sit back and hope that wealth will find you. Instead, take advantage of opportunities that come your way, and work at creating some opportunities yourself. Whether that means more networking, socializing, or education, you need to put in the required effort if you want to reach your goals. You also must believe in your ability to succeed. So the next time something good happens to you, take note and ask yourself why it happened. Chances are *you* did something to create that good fortune. Continue that self-propelling pattern, and that check with all the zeros may just land in your bank account one day.

(9–14 points)
### Fortune Is Far-Off

Feeling down on your luck? Unfortunately, it's all too obvious. Your lack of self-confidence is liable to ruin your chances of success. Because you often believe you don't have much to offer the world and don't feel worthy of good fortune, you hold back when it comes to expressing yourself and your opinions and trying to get things you want—such as a new job, a promotion, or even a date. The sooner you snap out of it, the better—for you and your bank balance! You need to get out there and get noticed, build your self-confidence, and take some chances in life while going after what you want. Opportunities will not come find you; you have to find and create opportunities for yourself. That's the key to living a rich life, in more ways than one.

# What Ice Cream Flavor Are You?

A pint of your favorite ice cream can speak gallons about your character. Loosely based on the science of "flavorology," this fun quiz can tell you all about your ice cream personality—and which flavor you're most compatible with in romance!

**1** **In your free time, you're most likely to be found**

____ **a.** Lounging at home or at the beach, doing nothing

____ **b.** Writing, drawing, or doing something creative

____ **c.** Reading a great book in a secluded spot

____ **d.** With friends at a favorite hangout

____ **e.** What free time?

**2** **Your idea of indulgence is**

____ **a.** A full day at a spa: facial, massage, the works

____ **b.** A feast at an expensive restaurant

____ **c.** A new pair of stylish but sensible shoes

____ **d.** A spontaneous trip to someplace new

____ **e.** Allowing yourself to have dessert

**3** **Your desktop is**

____ **a.** Crowded with pictures of family and loved ones

____ **b.** Imposingly stark—clutter is a weakness you refuse to give in to

____ **c.** A bit messy

____ **d.** Organized in a special system that makes sense only to you

____ **e.** Piled neatly with important projects

**4** **You take risks**

____ **a.** In love—you're a romantic

____ **b.** In your career—you're a go-getter

____ **c.** Rarely, if at all

____ **d.** In all areas of your life—you love to take chances

____ **e.** Only when you've carefully weighed the consequences

**5** **Your friends come to you for advice about**

____ **a.** Romance

____ **b.** Going after their dreams

____ **c.** Just about everything—you're a dependable confidante

____ **d.** Coping with change and new experiences

____ **e.** Getting their lives in order and on track

**6** **Your dream vacation is**

____ **a.** Decadent and relaxing—a Caribbean island

____ **b.** Adventurous and unusual—a hike in the rain forest

____ **c.** Quiet and soothing—a retreat in the country

____ **d.** Exhilarating and spontaneous—a whirlwind tour of a foreign city

____ **e.** Inspiring and uncomplicated—a road trip or a sail

**7** **At parties, you generally**

____ **a.** End up flirting with someone

____ **b.** End up in charge of the music, or leading a group conversation

____ **c.** End up in the kitchen—you're a little shy

____ **d.** Circulate widely and meet lots of new people

____ **e.** Help out the host or hostess

**8** **A long-time crush confesses feelings for you, but you're dating someone else. You**

____ **a.** Are moved by the romantic gesture and give in to temptation—figuring that one kiss couldn't hurt

____ **b.** Calculate how quickly you could dump your current significant other

____ **c.** Firmly tell your crush that it's impossible for you to consider betraying anyone

____ **d.** Are intrigued, flattered, and totally unsure of what to do

____ **e.** Feel surprised, but gracefully tell your crush that you're already involved

**9** **You're most proud of**

____ **a.** Your wonderful relationships with your family and friends

____ **b.** Your independence, creativity, and ambition

____ **c.** Your trustworthiness and the high standards you set for yourself

____ **d.** Your imagination, energy, and spirit

____ **e.** Your intelligence and down-to-earth good sense

# Scoring

Add up the number of As, Bs, Cs, Ds, and Es you chose. Find the category in which you had the most responses to determine your ice cream personality—and learn what that reveals about the real you. Also check out your secondary ice cream personality, based on your next highest number of responses.

(Mostly As)
## Chocolate

Chocolate ice cream types are flirtatious, charming, and even a little dramatic. No doubt you're an intuitive and sensitive person who puts a high value on family, relationships, and romance. But your instincts may sometimes steer you wrong: You tend to be easily influenced in directions that you know aren't the best for you, and you have a tendency toward self-indulgence. Still, your liveliness and your trusting nature have earned you many admirers and friends. Chocolate types are compatible with reliable Butter Pecans and high-focus, high-energy Chocolate Chips.

*Fun fact:* Chocolate is the second most popular ice cream flavor.

(Mostly Bs)
## Chocolate Chip

Chocolate Chip ice cream types are a creative force to be reckoned with. No doubt you've got a competitive streak a mile wide. The good news is that it brings out the best in you by forcing you to live up to your own demanding standards. Still, you can be rather unforgiving at times with those who don't share your vision and drive. Friends value your magnetism, charm, and originality. Chocolate Chips are best off with high-achieving Butter Pecans and empathetic, insightful Chocolates.

*Fun fact:* Chocolate chip ice cream lovers often also indulge in other "chunky" flavors, such as Cookie Dough, Mint Chip, and Rocky Road.

(Mostly Cs)
## Strawberry

Strawberry ice cream types are naturally loyal, honest, and trustworthy. No doubt you have a devoted circle of friends who rely on you for the right answer to any moral dilemma. Like Chocolate Chip types, you tend to set high standards for yourself, but you are somewhat shy and reserved. You don't like to admit it, but you're also a tad pessimistic. Maybe you're just disappointed that no one can seem to live up to your own sense of responsibility and forthrightness. Strawberry types do well with optimistic, outgoing Chocolate Chips.

*Fun fact:* Strawberry is tied with Butter Pecan as the third most popular ice cream flavor.

### (Mostly Ds)
## Vanilla

Contrary to what you may expect, Vanilla ice cream types aren't bland or boring. If this is your category, you're probably quite gregarious, impulsive, fun loving, and expressive. You may have a difficult time making up your mind—Vanillas are known for never saying no, even when they probably should. Vanilla types also tend to take a romantic, hopeful view of life. Your motto: Live for the moment, and everything will work out fine. Vanilla types are happiest with their own kind—only someone equally spontaneous and energetic will do.

*Fun fact:* Vanilla is far and away the most popular ice cream flavor.

### (Mostly Es)
## Butter Pecan

Butter Pecan ice cream types are organized, put-together, and generally valued for their fairness, efficiency, and lack of pretension—you won't see a Butter Pecan type putting on airs. It may be difficult for a no-nonsense Butter Pecan type like you to express yourself at all, even though you're privately quite sympathetic and observant. No doubt you like to plan ahead and take charge, which means you're often overcommitted. You're most compatible with your own kind—other Butter Pecan types who appreciate hard work and good sense.

*Fun fact:* Butter Pecan is tied with Strawberry for the third most popular ice cream flavor.

# What Do Your Dreams Reveal about You?

Are your dreams sending you a mysterious message? If you're curious about what your subconscious mind is trying to tell you, take this test and find out. (Call to mind those dreams you remember from the past few weeks.)

**1** The last time you woke up after a vivid dream, you felt

____ **a.** Scared or panicked

____ **b.** Tranquil or inspired

____ **c.** Emotional or enraged

____ **d.** Confused or disoriented

**2** When you dream of money or possessions, the theme is usually

____ **a.** That you've become suddenly rich or suddenly poor

____ **b.** That you're broke and can't pay your bills

____ **c.** That you have a full wallet or are surrounded by valuable objects

____ **d.** That you're doing something desperate to get your hands on some cash

**3** When food or appetite plays a role in your dreams, you can be found

____ **a.** Feeling really hungry but, strangely, not eating anything

____ **b.** Eating freely to the point of satisfaction

____ **c.** Surrounded by food but unable to decide what to eat

____ **d.** Eating a lot of food but never feeling full

**4** When you're behind the wheel in your dreams, you are

____ **a.** Speeding along happily in a gorgeous sports car

____ **b.** Behind the wheel of a car with brakes that don't work

____ **c.** Approaching a fork in the road, unsure of which way to go

____ **d.** Venting your frustrations on a junk-mobile that won't start

**5** Lately you dream of sex that

____ **a.** Leaves you feeling satisfied physically and emotionally

____ **b.** Leaves you feeling bitter and unhappy with your partner

____ **c.** Results in pregnancy

____ **d.** Leaves you feeling scared or uncomfortable

**6** When water appears in your dreams, you see yourself

____ **a.** Being washed away by a strong current

____ **b.** In jeopardy, because in your dream you cannot swim

____ **c.** Breathing easily underwater

____ **d.** Struggling with a tranquil tide that suddenly becomes turbulent

**7** When you find yourself naked in your dreams, you usually

____ **a.** Feel free and uninhibited

____ **b.** Are struggling to put your clothes on—but nothing fits!

____ **c.** Are in a public place, feeling embarrassingly exposed

____ **d.** Are in public and acting irritable

**8** Animals appearing lately in your dreams have been

____ **a.** Wild, angry, and hostile

____ **b.** Changing form, morphing one into the next

____ **c.** Hunted or threatened

____ **d.** Playful and friendly

**9** The structure that appears most in your dreams is

____ **a.** Your home or a place that feels like home

____ **b.** A fortress or prison

____ **c.** An empty house or unfamiliar place

____ **d.** A cramped, cluttered basement or room

**10** When you fly in your dreams, you

____ **a.** Feel scared by the height and generally uneasy

____ **b.** Soar through the sky, feeling free and empowered

____ **c.** Feel frustrated that you can't fly faster or higher

____ **d.** Usually fall or crash to the ground

# Scoring

Give yourself the numerical value that matches each of your answers. Then add all 10 scores together and use your total score to find your result category.

1.  **a** – 3  **b** – 4  **c** – 1  **d** – 2
2.  **a** – 2  **b** – 3  **c** – 4  **d** – 1
3.  **a** – 1  **b** – 4  **c** – 2  **d** – 3
4.  **a** – 4  **b** – 3  **c** – 2  **d** – 1
5.  **a** – 4  **b** – 1  **c** – 2  **d** – 3
6.  **a** – 3  **b** – 1  **c** – 4  **d** – 2
7.  **a** – 4  **b** – 2  **c** – 3  **d** – 1
8.  **a** – 1  **b** – 2  **c** – 3  **d** – 4
9.  **a** – 4  **b** – 3  **c** – 2  **d** – 1
10. **a** – 2  **b** – 4  **c** – 1  **d** – 3

(34–40 points)
## On Top of the World

Your dreams reveal that you feel strong, confident, and in control. Maybe you recently found the love of your life, or perhaps your boss is finally rewarding you for the all the extra business you've been bringing into the office. Whatever the case, you feel secure with yourself and ready to take on any future challenges. Just remember that there are some things in life that we can never control—so if you slip from your pedestal of power from time to time, don't be too hard on yourself.

(26–33 points)
## Losing Your Grip

Your score reveals that you may be feeling powerless, anxious, and out of control these days. Maybe you recently lost your job, or perhaps you're struggling with the loss of a loved one. Whatever the case, you may be feeling like a human ping-pong ball, hit back and forth between problems that you can't influence or control. Your dreams may be trying to tell you that it's time to make that big decision you've been putting off or that you need to accept that you're going through a tough time. So try to relax, and remember that this confusing life phase will eventually pass.

(18–25 points)
## Dealing with Change

Did you recently start a new job, move, or alter the status of a relationship? Your dreams reveal that you may be dealing with issues rooted in transition. When we are dealing with change in our everyday lives, our dreams often reflect the related stress and struggle. Not only do our dreams alert us to problems in our life, they can also serve as a safe space in which to explore the changes taking place in your life. Your subconscious mind is aware of everything that is going on in your body. It tries to "talk" to you when you're awake, but that doesn't always work, and so this communication moves to your dreams. Look for the meanings in your dreams: See if you can match the theme of your dream to a major area of your life. Reconsider the dream and your emotions during it. This may help you figure out how the dream relates to your life and what it is trying to tell you.

(10–17 points)

## Angry under the Surface

You may have a lot of bottled-up anger and hostility that you're releasing through your dreams because you are unable to rid yourself of it in your daily life. Maybe you've been having trouble communicating your emotions to your partner, or perhaps you dislike your boss so much that you just want to scream. Whatever the case, you've got a lot of pent-up aggression. Your subconscious knows a lot about you that you don't, or maybe don't care to know. In dreams your subconscious tries to get this information across to you in whatever way necessary—and it's not always pleasant. To work out what's troubling you, try talking to a close friend, using exercise as an outlet, or simply writing in a journal. If you get some of those feelings out in the open, you may soon dream that you're lying peacefully on the beach!

**BONUS TIP:** You can use your dreams to help handle challenging situations in your life. At night, try asking yourself a question about a difficult issue you're dealing with, and allow your subconscious mind to answer it through your dreams. Have a pen and paper by your bed so that you can easily record the dream when you wake up.

# 2

# Learn about Your Love Style

**And improve your chances for happiness**

What's Your Kissing Style?

How Romantic Are You?

How Sexy Are You?

How Hot Is Your Sex Life?

Astrological Passion: What Kind of Lover Are You?

If Your Love Life Were a Movie, Which One Would It Be?

Do You Know How to Get What You Want in Love?

# What's Your Kissing Style?

How you kiss can say a lot about your personality, your sensuality, and your feelings for the person you're kissing. Are you a passionate kisser? Or are your lips more playful? Answer these questions to find out what message you send when you smooch.

**1** Which activity would most put you in the mood for lovemaking?

____ **a.** A sexy movie

____ **b.** Slow dancing cheek to cheek

____ **c.** A shared activity or fun evening out

**2** Public displays of affection are

____ **a.** Unnecessary—you'd rather show your affection for your lover in private, one on one

____ **b.** A fun way to show that you appreciate your lover while you're walking hand in hand or dancing at a party

____ **c.** A must—you like to show the whole world how much you love your man

**3** What's your favorite type of goodnight kiss?

____ **a.** A brief touch of lips—it builds tension before the real thing

____ **b.** A sweet, gentle smooch

____ **c.** A long, juicy, enticing kiss

**4** After an especially long kiss, you usually

____ **a.** Lean back and look lovingly into his eyes

____ **b.** Gasp for air and dive right in for another

____ **c.** Take a break to nibble his ear

**5** You've just eaten garlic and your man is moving in for a kiss. What do you do?

____ **a.** Go with it—in a few seconds he'll be too hot to notice your breath anyway!

____ **b.** Pop a mint in your mouth and ask him to hold you in his arms instead.

____ **c.** Make a joke of your garlic breath and tell him he'd better postpone the Romeo routine.

**6** When you kiss a man, your hands are usually

\_\_\_\_ **a.** Running playfully through his hair

\_\_\_\_ **b.** Wrapped around his neck, holding him close

\_\_\_\_ **c.** Caressing his face, stroking his back, or grabbing some other body part

**7** During a kiss, you would like it if your man

\_\_\_\_ **a.** Stopped to look deep into your eyes

\_\_\_\_ **b.** Stopped to gently kiss your nose, forehead, shoulder

\_\_\_\_ **c.** Ran his tongue inside your lips along your teeth

**8** For you, what elements are necessary for a truly great kiss?

\_\_\_\_ **a.** Desire and intensity

\_\_\_\_ **b.** Affection and joy

\_\_\_\_ **c.** Ambiance and the perfect moment

**9** Your favorite movie couple is

\_\_\_\_ **a.** Meg Ryan and Billy Crystal in *When Harry Met Sally*

\_\_\_\_ **b.** Demi Moore and Patrick Swayze in *Ghost*

\_\_\_\_ **c.** Ingrid Bergman and Humphrey Bogart in *Casablanca*

**10** When it comes to kissing, you

\_\_\_\_ **a.** Often make the first move—you like to be in control

\_\_\_\_ **b.** Rarely make the first move—you like your man to be in control

\_\_\_\_ **c.** Are comfortable making the first move, as long as he takes the lead sometimes

## Scoring

Give yourself the numerical value that matches each of your answers. Then add all 10 scores together and use your total score to find your result category.

1. a – 1  b – 2  c – 3
2. a – 2  b – 3  c – 1
3. a – 3  b – 2  c – 1
4. a – 2  b – 1  c – 3
5. a – 1  b – 2  c – 3
6. a – 3  b – 2  c – 1
7. a – 2  b – 3  c – 1
8. a – 1  b – 3  c – 2
9. a – 3  b – 2  c – 1
10. a – 1  b – 2  c – 3

(24–30 points)

## Playful Kisser

Kissing is a lot of fun for you. You like your kisses to be sweet, playful, and rather flirty. No doubt your personality closely matches your kissing style. While being flirty and playful can be fun, exciting, and appealing, don't let your intimacy style sabotage your love life. Turning a playful relationship into a meaningful, enduring romance can be difficult, especially if both of you get too comfortable keeping things light and breezy. You may want to ask yourself why you tend not to let your intimate moments grow passionate. Are you afraid to get too intense? Are you uncomfortable with your sexual side? Insecure about your lovemaking skills? If so, it's time to experiment with other intimacy styles. Get romantic. Be passionate! Let your man—and yourself—get to know what's going on in your heart.

(17–23 points)

## Romantic Kisser

You love romance and like to be intimate when the mood and the moment are just right—candles flickering, soft music playing, gourmet food and good wine flowing. No doubt this has made for many memorable moments. But while you're busy plotting and planning (or waiting for) those perfect kissing moments, you may be missing out on the spontaneous side of love and sex. Remember that spontaneity can lead to romance. An unplanned stroll through the park, an impromptu breakfast in bed, or a shared shower can lead to memorable moments—and will definitely spark up your love life! Kissing and cuddling even when the mood isn't quite right can create closeness and add intimacy to your relationship. So try kissing your man when he least expects it. Chances are he'll be pleasantly surprised, and you may unleash a new passionate side of your relationship.

(10–16 points)

## Passionate Kisser

You are an enthusiastic and intense kisser. You aren't afraid to throw caution to the wind and kiss like there's no tomorrow, and you don't hesitate to make the first move. Being passionate is an enviable gift—it's no secret that passionate people enjoy great sex lives. Plus you're obviously comfortable with your sexual side—another enviable quality.

But you may want to think about turning down the heat sometimes. With so much passion, there may be little room to make an emotional connection. While sex is important in a relationship, so is being able to relax, talk, and just have fun together—out of bed as well as in! And while most men love a passionate woman, remember that they like to be the sexual aggressors sometimes. So relax once in a while and let your man try out his moves. It's fun to be on the receiving end!

# How Romantic Are You?

Some people drip *l'amour* from every pore, while others would rather wax poetic about the joys of waxing the floor. Where do you fit in? Find out just how romantic you are and how that affects your love life.

**1** **What's your ideal way to spend an evening?**

____ **a.** Drinking champagne with your beloved

____ **b.** Painting the kitchen of your new home together

____ **c.** Cuddling with your dog

**2** **Imagine that the guy you've been seeing for one month proposes (hey, it could happen!). You**

____ **a.** Make him return the ring immediately, but not before breaking up with him

____ **b.** Squeal with delight and slide that rock on in record time

____ **c.** Tell him you're tempted but feel the two of you need to know each other better before taking such a big step

**3** **If you could view your life on DVD, what would it look like?**

____ **a.** *Casablanca*—your life is passionate and dramatic.

____ **b.** *Boys on the Side*—your life is fun and not overly focused on men.

____ **c.** The complete collection of *In the Kitchen with Martha* (as in, Stewart)—your life is filled with projects and practicality.

**4** **Which article of clothing would you be most eager to receive from your lover?**

____ **a.** The dress he knows you've had your eye on

____ **b.** Something sexy from Victoria's Secret

____ **c.** A gift certificate would be better

**5** **When it comes to blind dates, you think**

___ **a.** You might as well go—you won't do any better at a singles' bar

___ **b.** Sometimes they work, sometimes they don't

___ **c.** Kismet just might bring you together with your Mr. Right

**6** **What do you want most from a relationship?**

___ **a.** A partner who provides tons of fun and loving surprises

___ **b.** A companion to share life's ups and downs with

___ **c.** Someone you can still be friends with if you call it quits

**7** **Where is your dream honeymoon spot?**

___ **a.** An island in the Caribbean—it's private

___ **b.** Thailand—it's fascinating

___ **c.** Disney World—it's fun

**8** **Which card game would you be most likely to play with your honey?**

___ **a.** Strip Poker

___ **b.** Go Fish

___ **c.** War

**9** **What do you typically wear to bed?**

___ **a.** A cozy nightgown

___ **b.** Just a smile—or lacy lingerie

___ **c.** Sweatpants and a T-shirt

**10** **Of the following, which food would you rather eat?**

___ **a.** Oysters

___ **b.** Anything with garlic

___ **c.** Oatmeal or a whole-wheat bagel

**11** **What gift are you planning on giving your sweetie for Valentine's Day?**

___ **a.** Nothing special—Valentine's Day is just a day for the greeting card and floral industries to gouge couples.

___ **b.** The one thing he's been wishing for (CD, toolbox, shirt, whatever).

___ **c.** A love sonnet that could rival one written by Shakespeare.

**12** If you picked up the phone at your guy's apartment and heard him talking to a woman, you would instantly assume

___ **a.** He was talking to a female acquaintance—after all, you have plenty of *male* friends

___ **b.** He was cheating on you—the cad!

___ **c.** She is a friend of yours and he was planning a surprise party for you

# Scoring

Give yourself the numerical value that matches each of your answers. Then add all 12 scores together and use your total score to find your result category.

1. a – 3  b – 2  c – 1
2. a – 1  b – 3  c – 2
3. a – 3  b – 1  c – 2
4. a – 2  b – 3  c – 1
5. a – 1  b – 2  c – 3
6. a – 3  b – 2  c – 1
7. a – 3  b – 1  c – 2
8. a – 3  b – 2  c – 1
9. a – 2  b – 3  c – 1
10. a – 3  b – 1  c – 2
11. a – 1  b – 2  c – 3
12. a – 2  b – 1  c – 3

**(29–36 points)**

## Über-Romantic

To you the world is one big Harlequin novel—or it should be. You love, love, *love* all the romantic accoutrements: flowers, candy, moonlit dances, poetry, and more. Not for you is the notion that once a couple settles in it's okay if life together becomes routine. Your view is that lovers should always aim to keep a "snap, crackle, and pop" in their relationship. What's wonderful is that you will never take a man for granted. You will always wear sexy undies to bed, plan special birthday surprises, and harbor a yen for intimate candlelight conversations. But you have a tendency toward idealizing love. You do really need to get to know a person before proclaiming that the two of you are soul mates. And once you're a unit, don't expect your partner to always be in the mood to be Super Romantic Man. Sometimes he just wants to watch TV, grab fast food (versus a gourmet meal), or chill by himself in the den. This just says that he feels comfortable enough in the relationship to be himself. Now isn't *that* romantic?

(20–28 points)

## More Sensible Than Sensuous

You're more of an oatmeal and flannel kind of gal. The gestures that most touch your heart are those that prove your lover really listens—his buying you the dress you had your eye on versus splurging on a barely-there negligee you may never wear comfortably. You most enjoy shared endeavors (such as painting the kitchen of your new home). You have both feet on the ground, and don't see your guy as the be-all-and-end-all of your existence. It's important to you to have your own friends, work, and interests. This is healthy for your relationship (your man loves you more for it) and for your sense of independence and self-esteem. But occasionally let your "girlie" side come out to play. Every once in a while let him wine and dine you. Give him a romantic card or flowers on Valentine's Day along with the toolbox he's been yearning for. The best relationships are ones in which you're not only friends and companions but fun-loving, sensuous beings. He's your Romeo, not your roommate.

(12–19 points)

## One Tough Cookie

You're tough—or at least you try to be. But everyone knows that underneath that cynic's shell lies someone who still believes in love, romance, and all that jazz. It's wonderful that you have a strong sense of self and won't allow yourself to be swept away by pretty words and romantic promises. And you can enjoy some aspects of a not-perfect relationship—such as a trip to an exotic destination. It's not so wonderful that you expect a man to disappoint you (just because he's talking to another woman doesn't mean he's cheating!). The objective to strive for is to be cautious, not closed. Let a man prove himself trustworthy, and once that happens, trust him. Then enjoy his romantic gestures, and heck, make a few yourself.

# How Sexy Are You?

Some women make heads turn when they enter a room—not just because they're beautiful but because they possess that winning combination of charm, strength, and confidence that equals sex appeal. What sex vibes do *you* radiate? Take this test and find out if your powers of seduction are over the top, too tame, or just right.

**1** **When you kiss or make love, your eyes are usually**

____ **a.** Open—you like to watch how he's reacting

____ **b.** Closed—you feel too exposed when you leave them open

____ **c.** Closed—it's more intimate and cozy that way

**2** **If a TV character were based on you, she would be the**

____ **a.** Quiet and capable coworker who's tough to get to know

____ **b.** Confident and casual boss

____ **c.** Office flirt

**3** **Your underwear drawer contains:**

____ **a.** Pretty panties, at least one Miracle-type bra, and several lacy undergarments that are more about form than function

____ **b.** Cotton panties, basic bras (no padding, little lace), and maybe an old teddy you didn't even remember you had

____ **c.** A considerable collection of Victoria's Secret's sexiest attire

**4** **To you, talking dirty in bed**

____ **a.** Is a must—after all, men like it

____ **b.** Can be fun and stimulating if the mood and the man are right

____ **c.** Isn't going to happen in your bedroom anytime soon

**5** **When a man tells you that you look great, what is your typical response?**

____ **a.** "Thank you."

____ **b.** "Really? Do you think so?"

____ **c.** "Ugh, no, I don't, I look terrible."

**6** You like it when men think of you as

____ **a.** Smart and stable

____ **b.** Passionate and romantic

____ **c.** Mysterious and a little dangerous

**7** While dining with friends, you notice that a nice-looking guy at the next table keeps looking your way. What do you do?

____ **a.** Give him your best come-hither look

____ **b.** Return his look with a smile

____ **c.** Hope he comes over to speak to you

**8** You're going to the office holiday party. What do you wear?

____ **a.** A classic black dress and a pair of dressy pumps

____ **b.** The same type of outfit you wear every day, plus a colorful scarf for a touch of festivity

____ **c.** A slim-fitting dress and your highest heels—it's party time!

**9** Your fingernails can best be described as

____ **a.** Cat's claws

____ **b.** Neat 'n' nude

____ **c.** Bitten to the bone

**10** You and some girlfriends decide to go to a dance club. How long does it take to get you out on the dance floor?

____ **a.** Dance floor? Who said anything about dancing?

____ **b.** That depends on how long it takes you to drag a guy out there.

____ **c.** About as long as it takes to walk from the door to the floor, partner or not.

**11** You know your body and what pleases you sexually about as well as you know

____ **a.** The inner workings of your VCR

____ **b.** The back of your hand

____ **c.** The color of your eyes

**12** Your idea of kinky sex is

____ **a.** Doing it with the lights on

____ **b.** Doing it on a weeknight

____ **c.** Tying a guy to the bedpost

**⑬ When undressing in front of a man, your style most resembles**

____ **a.** A striptease act

____ **b.** Your daily disrobing routine

____ **c.** A run for the covers

**⑭ When it comes to sex, you make the first move**

____ **a.** Most of the time—you like to be the leader

____ **b.** Less than 25 percent of the time—you don't want to scare him off

____ **c.** About 50 percent of the time—you try to show him that you're as interested as he is

# Scoring

Give yourself the numerical value that matches each of your answers. Then add all 14 scores together and use your total score to find your result category.

1. a – 3  b – 1  c – 2
2. a – 1  b – 2  c – 3
3. a – 2  b – 1  c – 3
4. a – 3  b – 2  c – 1
5. a – 2  b – 3  c – 1
6. a – 1  b – 2  c – 3
7. a – 3  b – 2  c – 1
8. a – 2  b – 1  c – 3
9. a – 3  b – 2  c – 1
10. a – 1  b – 3  c – 2
11. a – 1  b – 2  c – 3
12. a – 2  b – 1  c – 3
13. a – 3  b – 2  c – 1
14. a – 3  b – 1  c – 2

**(34–42 points)**

## Serious Seductress

You've got sex appeal all right, but you may be overdoing it. Going after guys with the hard sell isn't likely to lead to a healthy, long-lasting relationship. Your *femme fatale* act may backfire. Those desperation vibes may push guys away. Cleavage-exposing blouses, slinky skirts, and come-hither looks may have guys flocking to you like they do to *Monday Night Football*, but their interest is likely to diminish soon after the first, uh, touchdown. If you want men to get to know you (and not just your body), tone down the super-sexy routine and work on developing true sex appeal—confidence, poise, and a positive attitude. Ask yourself why you feel the need to portray yourself as such a sexual dynamo. Some women are afraid that their other qualities aren't attractive enough, or that all men want is a woman whose appearance and behavior scream "sex." But when it comes to long-term relationships, men want a woman who is confident and comfortable with herself, whom they enjoy spending time with, can relax with and respect, and are attracted to—on the outside *and* in.

## (24–33 points)
## Sufficiently Sexy

You tend to engage men more with your personality and confidence than with your looks. Not that you don't care about your appearance—you do. But your style is more casual and classy than dressed-to-impress. Men feel comfortable around you, probably because they can tell how comfortable you are with yourself. You draw them in without overwhelming them. That's great, but don't be afraid to act alluring sometimes, too. As long as you know when to draw the line and let men see and appreciate your nonphysical qualities, it can be fun to play up your sexuality.

## (14–23 points)
## Too Tame

Your sex appeal seems to be in hiding. Men tend to think of you more as a friend than a lover, especially since the vibes you give off are often on the cool side. Granted, your life is busy, but you may be suppressing your natural sex appeal for other reasons. You may not be comfortable in your "sexual skin," or past rejections or heartbreaks have led you to put up your guard. Or you may be uncomfortable with your body or looks. To improve your love life, battle your fears and insecurities and get in touch with your sexual side. Boost your self-esteem by taking up an activity that makes you feel good (a writing class, a race-walking program, and so on). If your low self-esteem is deep-rooted, consider professional counseling or personal development seminars. Practice positive self-talk in the car, in front of the mirror, as a before-bed ritual. Tell yourself what an attractive, sexy, smart woman you are, and soon you will believe it—as well you should. Sex appeal is not about looks. It's about exuding confidence, style, and smarts.

# How Hot Is Your Sex Life?

Take this between-the-sheets test to find out how you score in the bedroom—and learn how to turn up the heat.

**❶ How long does your lovemaking typically last, foreplay through climax?**

____ **a.** Fifteen minutes or less—your crazy schedule doesn't allow for much more.

____ **b.** One hour or more—you like to go slow; besides, one time isn't usually enough.

____ **c.** In the 30-minute range—just enough time for both of you to (usually) feel fulfilled.

**❷ When it comes to discussing sex with a partner, you**

____ **a.** Offer lots of "hints"—you're not always comfortable talking about sex, but you might move his hand or show him a new position

____ **b.** Often initiate discussion—you want to share your desires, fantasies, even your complaints

____ **c.** Rarely speak up—you're not comfortable discussing your desires with anyone

**❸ The last time you had sex, your mind was on**

____ **a.** Your pleasure and your partner's

____ **b.** A handsome movie actor or other male fantasy figure

____ **c.** All the errands and chores you needed to do

**❹ Which of the following have you done in the past month?**

____ **a.** Worn silky underwear—not that anyone noticed it

____ **b.** Worn silky underwear—and made sure your partner noticed it

____ **c.** Worn silky underwear—and stripped it off in front of your partner

**❺ Your idea of perfect sex is**

____ **a.** When both of you climax

____ **b.** Doing it before you're too exhausted to enjoy it

____ **c.** Doing something experimental in the bedroom and finding that it intensifies the experience

**6** Your lover thinks foreplay begins when he

____ **a.** Kisses you deeply while caressing your face, hair, and body

____ **b.** Turns off the TV

____ **c.** Comes to bed without his pajamas on

**7** When your lover is undressing before sex, you are usually

____ **a.** Helping him

____ **b.** Watching and enjoying the "show"

____ **c.** Reminding him to hang up his clothes

**8** How often do you have an orgasm during sex?

____ **a.** Hardly ever

____ **b.** Almost all the time

____ **c.** Often but not all the time

**9** Your night table drawer contains

____ **a.** Massage oil and scented candles

____ **b.** The book you're currently reading

____ **c.** Handcuffs or another sex toy

**10** Your best friend is in a new, passion-filled relationship. When she fills you in on the sexy details, you

____ **a.** Can't help feeling jealous—you wish you and your honey could be that way together again

____ **b.** Vow to yourself that you'll turn up the heat this weekend

____ **c.** Share a few of your own sexy details with her

## Scoring

Give yourself the numerical value that matches each of your answers. Then add all 10 scores together and use your total score to find your result category.

1. a – 1  b – 3  c – 2
2. a – 2  b – 3  c – 1
3. a – 3  b – 2  c – 1
4. a – 1  b – 2  c – 3
5. a – 2  b – 1  c – 3
6. a – 3  b – 1  c – 2
7. a – 2  b – 3  c – 1
8. a – 1  b – 3  c – 2
9. a – 2  b – 1  c – 3
10. a – 1  b – 2  c – 3

(24–30 points)
## Your Sex Life Is Sizzling

For you, sex is an exciting adventure—all about passion and mutual satisfaction. There may be no place you would rather be than wrapped in a tight embrace. You know how to please your man, and you clearly communicate your sexual needs and wants. And while you don't need experimentation to make your love life hot, you like to try new things, especially when you're feeling bored with your usual routine. Many women dream of having your energy, spontaneity, and lack of inhibition. You may, however, find that your intense focus on extreme passion, lusty behavior, and physical pleasures distract you from other important elements you may desire in your relationship, such as emotional closeness and friendship. If that's the case, devote some time to connecting on other levels beyond the physical.

(17–23 points)
## Your Sex Life Is Simmering

You aren't consumed by a passionate need for a bedroom romp every night, but you do enjoy sex, especially with a long-term mate you love and trust. And while you aren't a wild woman between the sheets, you're not entirely inhibited, either. You know that physical connection is often the best way to connect emotionally. All the more reason to vow not to let too much time pass between "sex nights." It's natural for you and your partner to hit slow patches—the frequency and enjoyment of most couples' sexual contact wanes over time, especially with the intense daily demands of today's world. But be sure to make time for sexual pleasure, which can include massaging each other, sharing a shower, or cuddling under the covers. This kind of connection, even if it doesn't involve intercourse, can enhance your life and your relationship.

(10–16 points)
## Your Sex Life Is Humdrum

Your sex life has fallen into a lull. If you have a man in your life, perhaps you two have fallen into a sexual routine that just doesn't cut it for one or both of you. Or maybe the demands of daily life have taken a toll on your libido. You may also be experiencing a common cooling off in bed—typical for lovers in long-term relationships. At times like this, it's important to work on improving your sexual connection. Spark up your love life with some lacy lingerie, or bring your favorite food to bed and attempt a little experimentation. Don't be afraid to expect pleasure—allowing your mate to please you will make him feel great. Most importantly, talk to your partner about what you need in bed, and find out what he desires. Communication and trust are important tools for unlocking the sexual diva inside you.

# Astrological Passion: What Kind of Lover Are You?

Do you know exactly what gets you in the mood and why? The key to your physical passion—and a satisfying sex life!—may be hidden in the stars. Whatever your Sun Sign, you most likely display a mixture of energies based on how the four astrological Elements (Fire, Water, Earth, and Air) configure themselves in your chart. Finding out which Elements rule your physical passions can help you to know what sort of lovers you attract and how you can have a great sex life. Answer these questions and discover your sexual turn-ons and talents!

**1** **What do you require in the way of foreplay?**

____ **a.** Foreplay, *shmoreplay*—you just like to be taken!

____ **b.** Romantic music, candlelight, and time—you don't like to rush this kind of thing.

____ **c.** You need the works, and you like it when one thing leads naturally to another—tender shoulder massages that lead to soft, slow kisses that lead to ear-nibbling that lead to . . .

____ **d.** As long as you and your lover have been swapping stories and sharing laughter, you're good to go.

**2** **What's your biggest turn-on in a potential sexual partner?**

____ **a.** You can't resist someone natural, with an easygoing but confident presence.

____ **b.** You swoon for someone with a witty, self-deprecating sense of humor.

____ **c.** You're drawn to mystery, someone you can't quite figure out—you want to explore that darkness.

____ **d.** You're a sucker for a hot body.

**3** **When it comes time to turn on the charm, which seduction tricks do you use?**

____ **a.** You lure your sweetie into your tricky little web of wit, humor, and innuendo, your words whipping him into a fervent frenzy.

_____ **b.** You appeal to your lover's senses with slow, sensual touch and silky, sophisticated lingerie.

_____ **c.** You act spirited and passionate, willing to please but never submissive.

_____ **d.** You tune yourself into your lover's feelings—if your moods sync, your bodies will follow.

**4** **Which would you say is your most erogenous zone?**

_____ **a.** Your skin

_____ **b.** Your mind

_____ **c.** Your heart

_____ **d.** You are a walking, talking erogenous zone

**5** **What are your biggest turn-offs?**

_____ **a.** Wimps

_____ **b.** Baby talk

_____ **c.** Men who don't read

_____ **d.** Sarcastic or overly cynical hipsters

**6** **If you had to choose an animal to personify your animal nature, you would be a:**

_____ **a.** Charming and playful puppy

_____ **b.** Cuddly, loving kitten

_____ **c.** Wild horse

_____ **d.** Powerful and protective tigress

**7** **Your lover is feeling playful and adventurous. Which of the following intimacy venues would you consider?**

_____ **a.** You and your lover and the warm jets of a backyard hot tub sounds too good to resist.

_____ **b.** Well, you've always kind of fantasized about that "mile-high club" thing.

_____ **c.** You'd contemplate a lusty roll on a secluded beach, but you'd have to be assured it was secluded!

_____ **d.** You're open to anywhere, anytime.

**8** **How do you feel about discussing sex with your partner?**

_____ **a.** You don't want to waste time talking about it—you just want to get to it!

_____ **b.** It's a must between responsible adults; you have to make sure you and your partner are involved for the same reasons.

_____ **c.** Talking about it excites you. You love getting all those sordid details out into the open.

_____ **d.** You don't mind hearing your lover's needs and desires, but you're a bit reticent about sharing your own thoughts and fantasies.

**9** If your mind wanders during the act, whom would you most likely imagine as your dream desert-island-superstar lover?

____ **a.** George Clooney

____ **b.** Benicio Del Toro

____ **c.** Russell Crowe

____ **d.** Matt Damon

**10** What could your partner do to make your sex life more enjoyable?

____ **a.** Take more initiative—you would love to be surprised by a spontaneous indecent proposal!

____ **b.** Slow things down—rushing it does not turn you on.

____ **c.** Stop trying to talk you into having sex. When you're not in the mood, you're just not in the mood—the pressure and guilt just turn you right off.

____ **d.** Be more sensitive to your needs and desires.

## Scoring

Give yourself the numerical value that matches each of your answers. Then add all 10 scores together and use your total score to find your result category.

1. a – 4  b – 1  c – 3  d – 2
2. a – 3  b – 2  c – 1  d – 4
3. a – 2  b – 3  c – 4  d – 1
4. a – 3  b – 2  c – 1  d – 4
5. a – 4  b – 3  c – 2  d – 1
6. a – 2  b – 1  c – 4  d – 3
7. a – 1  b – 2  c – 3  d – 4
8. a – 4  b – 3  c – 2  d – 1
9. a – 3  b – 1  c – 4  d – 2
10. a – 4  b – 3  c – 2  d – 1

(34–40 points)

### Ardent Fire Sign Lover

You share your sexuality with others with all the passion and confidence of the Fire Signs. Impulsive, playful, and irresistible, you bound into new romantic entanglements hungry for pleasure and attention. You crave constant physical stimulation and can be quite daring and experimental in the bedroom. You're very *me*-oriented, so you may sometimes forget your partner's wants and needs or take him for granted. However, you can also be incredibly generous when it comes to giving sexual pleasure. You're willing to take risks with your heart and pay no mind to consequences.

*Turn-on tips:* Be bold like an Aries, and enticing and exuberant like a Leo. And just like adventurous, devil-may-care Sagittarius, tease your lover until neither of you can stand it anymore!

## (26–33 points)
### Sensual Earth Sign Lover

Your sexual expression is of an Earth Sign nature. Realistic, grounded, and patient, you are straightforward in conveying your desire. You value your time and your energy, so you don't want to waste any playing games with your affections. In your eyes, honest intimacy is the best policy—that way, you keep a firm grasp on the consequences of your actions and decisions. You realize that sex has mental, emotional, and physical implications. But that doesn't mean you don't know how to enjoy yourself! Earth Sign energy is highly responsive to touch and sensation.

*Turn-on tips:* Channel Taurus's slow and sensuous vibe and, like a Virgo or Capricorn, show meticulous care for creating a pleasurable experience and ensuring that your lover's needs are met.

## (18–25 points)
### Flirty Air Sign Lover

Your sexuality comes through in the way you communicate—through your gestures and your inventive ideas—just like an Air Sign. To you sex is simply another way to connect and share energy with your fellow humans. While you're exceptionally expressive, you may downplay your own emotions in romantic relationships, keeping an aloof distance as a defense against getting hurt. That's not to say that you're no fun between the sheets. Quite to the contrary, you're a playful, flirtatious lover, stimulated by the interplay of two personalities and by some degree of light-hearted debate. A little dirty talk and some intellectual fireworks will keep you aroused!

*Turn-on tips:* Entice and tempt like a mischievous Gemini and turn on the magnetic charm of a Libra. Like gregarious Aquarius, spice things up with experimental new techniques.

## (10–17 points)
### Sensitive Water Sign Lover

You're more soulful than the average lover and, like a Water Sign, your physical yearnings are inextricably tied to your emotions. You feel things deeply and may tend to idealize lovers, hoping with each intimate encounter that you've finally found your soul mate, who understands your intense, complex heart and fulfills your fantasies. Your vivid imagination and strong emotional attachments can intimidate some, but your profound and unguarded response to intimacy is worth the risk. Because you're so openhearted, you're also vulnerable to opportunists. You would do well to take some advice from Cancer and steel yourself with emotional armor.

*Turn-on tips:* Surprise and delight with the bold sexual creativity of Scorpio, and like dreamy Pisces, express to your lover the depth of your pleasure. He will appreciate knowing the impact he's had on you!

# If Your Love Life Were a Movie, Which One Would It Be?

Whether it's a true romance or a tearjerker, chances are that your love life follows the same story line of one of seven different silver screen hits. Take this test and find out which movie your love life mimics most, what that says about your romantic patterns, and what's in store for your real-life relationships.

**1** **Which of the following best describes the way you and your most recent love interest met?**

____ **a.** You were at a bar and you saw him checking you out from his dark corner.

____ **b.** He is or was your supervisor at work.

____ **c.** You admit it—after spotting him, you made sure that the two of you "accidentally" bumped into each other.

____ **d.** At an event where he was the keynote speaker/honoree.

____ **e.** Through a friend, but you had a boyfriend at the time.

____ **f.** You were both at a self-improvement seminar or continuing education class.

____ **g.** You were friends for a long time before he finally convinced you to try dating.

**2** **What's your idea of the perfect first date?**

____ **a.** Doing something daring that you wouldn't normally do, like going for a motorcycle ride, hang gliding, or even skydiving.

____ **b.** Attending a wine tasting on a beautiful vineyard (even better, he'd teach you some wine tips along the way!).

____ **c.** It's been so long since you've been out, you would think anything was perfect as long as it was a date!

____ **d.** An evening of wining, dining, and dancing at a charity ball—paid for by your date, of course.

____ **e.** A *perfect* date? That's asking way too much. You'll settle for a *good* date, doing just about anything—you're not particular.

____ **f.** You'd cook him a delicious dinner and send him home with leftovers that he'll love.

____ **g.** Drinks at a local bar—something casual and low-key, without high expectations.

**3** **When it's time to celebrate your significant other's birthday, you would be most likely to**

____ **a.** Buy him something racy (not a typical gift you'd give at all)—when else would you get to shop for something like that?

____ **b.** Get him a first edition of his favorite book, which he told you about

____ **c.** Put together a scrapbook for him, including recent photos, ticket stubs, and other dating memorabilia that you've collected

____ **d.** Splurge on a quality gift you hope will meet his high standards

____ **e.** Buy him whatever he wants most no matter how difficult it is to get—you only want to please him

____ **f.** Buy him a new outfit you know he'd never buy on his own—it's the perfect chance to get him to ditch those ratty old jeans

____ **g.** Get him something nice, but not too nice—you don't want him to think you're more serious about him than you really are

**4** **If you were hoping to make a match using the personals, which ad would be most likely to catch your eye?**

____ **a.** Rebel with a Cause seeks SF to run away, live on the edge, and see the world

____ **b.** Man of the World seeks fellow student of life to read, travel, cook, and more

____ **c.** Don't Let This One Get Away! SM seeking lifetime partner ASAP

____ **d.** Professional Male looking for lovely lady to enjoy the finer things in life

____ **e.** Long Distance Love Affair? Busy professional hoping to fill limited free hours with passion—but only with the right woman

____ **f.** Average Joe looking for caring, compassionate woman to teach me everything you know about love—I'm a great student!

____ **g.** Guy Looking for Girl for fun, laughs, and no mention of the M word

**5** **In a past life, you most likely would have been a**

____ **a.** Star-crossed lover, like Juliet

____ **b.** Lady who became a princess, like Diana

____ **c.** Passionate, misunderstood soul, like Joan of Arc

____ **d.** First Lady, like Jackie Kennedy

____ **e.** Holy woman, like Mother Theresa

____ **f.** Caretaker, like Florence Nightingale

____ **g.** Successful and independent woman, like Jane Austen

**6** **If you asked her to be truly honest, what would your best friend say about your current mate (or your last boyfriend)?**

\_\_\_\_ **a.** "He's not right for you."

\_\_\_\_ **b.** "Isn't he a bit old for you?"

\_\_\_\_ **c.** "You're spending an awful lot of time together."

\_\_\_\_ **d.** "He's like a king! Does he have a brother?"

\_\_\_\_ **e.** "You're so lucky to have such a solid, loyal guy."

\_\_\_\_ **f.** "I guess he has potential."

\_\_\_\_ **g.** "He seems like a great guy. You should give it a chance!"

**7** **The men you fall for are usually**

\_\_\_\_ **a.** Your opposite

\_\_\_\_ **b.** Older and wiser than you

\_\_\_\_ **c.** Hard to catch

\_\_\_\_ **d.** Powerful and put-together

\_\_\_\_ **e.** Romantic but unavailable

\_\_\_\_ **f.** Diamonds in the rough

\_\_\_\_ **g.** Nice but no one you're ready to settle down with

## Scoring

Add up the number of As, Bs, Cs, Ds, Es, Fs, and Gs you chose. Look for the category in which you had the most choices to find the movie your love life mimics most—and learn what that says about your romantic patterns. Also check out the other movies that influence your love life, based on your responses.

(Mostly As)

### Your Love Life Is Like *Dirty Dancing*

Like Jennifer Grey's character in this movie, you tend to fall for guys from the wrong side of the tracks, or at least the *other* side of the tracks. Your version of Johnny Castle, the smoldering dance instructor played by Patrick Swayze, may come from a different socioeconomic class or merely want very different things out of life than you do.

But the question is if this type of guy really fulfills your needs. If you find yourself jumping into relationships with one bad boy after another, it may be time to do some self-assessment and uncover the reasons why. Your habit of choosing such mates may relate to your relationship with your parents—and your need to establish your independence from them. Even if you admire your parents (and their marriage), breaking free of any expectations is important to you, and your relationship choices reflect that. Once you deal with the effects that your parents and their relationship had on you, you may have an easier time finding a man with qualities that will make you truly happy—someone with whom you can share a long-term, healthy, and grown-up relationship.

## (Mostly Bs)
### Your Love Life Is Like *My Fair Lady*

You could probably strongly identify with the plot of this and movies with similar themes, such as *Working Girl, Educating Rita,* and *Annie Hall*: a younger woman falls in love with an older male mentor. Your desire to mix romance with wisdom may stem from feeling that you didn't get enough guidance from your parents or teachers in your youth. Now you're hoping to make a match with an accomplished professional who can show you the ropes (among other things). Many men enjoy this situation because it allows them to relive their rise to the top. But while it's easy to fall for someone you admire, this type of relationship eventually will need a level playing field to stay strong. You'll need to find other things that you love about him, beyond what he can teach you. Likewise, he should show you how much he respects you—not only for what you've accomplished but also for who you were every step of the way. Only when you both learn to see each other as equals can your love become enduring.

## (Mostly Cs)
### Your Love Life Is Like *Fatal Attraction*

Relationships are intense for you. Like Glenn Close's character in this movie, you might be a generous and passionate lover, but falling for men in an obsessive way leads to trouble. Chances are breakups are especially painful for you. You may have a difficult time establishing the natural boundaries of a healthy relationship. You may be giving so much of yourself to your partner and the relationship that losing either one becomes unbearable. Letting go—and accepting that the relationship is over—is a challenge because your self-esteem is wrapped up in something that is no longer available. The good news is that you have the power to change your story line, and the first step is realizing your own worth. Nearly everyone gets off course at some point, and it's common to think that the only possible solution is the help—or the love—of another person.

But this isn't true. It may be time to start dealing with why you feel that you need a man in your life to feel good about yourself. Consider self-help books, therapy, or simply talking things through with a close friend. No matter which method you choose, the objective is the same: to learn to admire and appreciate yourself.

## (Mostly Ds)
### Your Love Life Is Like *Pretty Woman*

Cinderella may be your favorite fairy-tale heroine, but there is more to your story than a magical pumpkin carriage and the search for Prince Charming. For starters, you may have felt misunderstood growing up. That's why you love the idea of a busy and powerful man taking the time to really get to know and appreciate you. Your fondness for a guy who is successful but distant may also stem from your relationship with your own father. If he was cold to you or rejected you as a child, you may be trying to overcome feelings of unworthiness by bonding with another equally intimidating man. If the men you are usually attracted to come from more distinguished backgrounds than you, your objective may be to win them over with your charm, passion, and wit. You want

to prove that your traits and talents are just as valuable as their money and education. Be careful that you're not trying to rewrite your father-daughter story: Even if it's only subconscious, a woman who places too much value on finding—and fixing—a man with the same characteristics as her father runs the risk of repeating the same painful experiences all over again. It may be time to examine your true motivation for choosing a mate. Plenty of women fall for men who remind them of dear old Dad, but your romantic relationships should be based on your grown-up needs. Concentrate on what you want now and in the future, and let the past stay in the past.

## (Mostly Es)
### Your Love Life Is Like *Casablanca*

You are practical and traditional—even when it comes to romance. You like to keep your emotions under control, and you're not one to rock the boat. Like Ingrid Bergman's character in this movie, relationships have meant sacrifice to you because you've put passion second to things like pride, duty, and family obligations. It's a common theme in movies such as *The Bridges of Madison County*: The leading lady marries a man who offers stability, only to fall deeply and intensely in love with another. You may believe that the pursuit of a love interest who is "off limits" will destroy the comfortable life that you've worked so hard to create for yourself. Even the mere temptation to get involved is enough to make you feel guilty. You don't want to risk causing pain to others. While the high standards you've set for yourself are commendable, you may be holding yourself back from happiness in the long run. Women who put the needs of others before their own often end up regretting their decisions and in some cases resenting the very people whom they were trying to spare pain. No one is recommending adultery, but be sure that your motivation for your decisions is based on what you truly want to get out of life—*your* life.

## (Mostly Fs)
## Your Love Life Is Like *Beauty and the Beast*

In your eyes, nothing sparkles more than a diamond in the rough. Like the heroine in this story, you tend to fall for guys whom others have overlooked

or misunderstood. They just can't see the potential that you do. But your motivation for molding and shaping a prospective Mr. Right isn't as self-destructive as you might think—or as your friends probably say it is. Instead, it may be the result of your wish to be "rescued" yourself. The most satisfying relationships for you are those where you and your partner both challenge and inspire each other to be the very best versions of yourselves. In such a relationship, you feel needed—and he feels like a hero. Not a bad ending, right?

## (Mostly Gs)
## Your Love Life is Like *My Best Friend's Wedding*

While you may have many dates or short-term relationships, your fear of commitment has kept you from pursuing a lasting relationship. Your friends may be marching down the aisle, but you probably still consider yourself "not ready," possibly because of a fear of growing up and growing old. But like Julia Roberts' character in this movie, sooner or later you'll realize that you will not live forever. The plot line for stories like this revolves around the moment when a person recognizes that she has a finite amount of time to live the life and share the love that she wants to. Eventually you'll learn to get past your fears and understand that avoiding or postponing intimacy isn't going to keep you young or enrich your life. When you do fall in love, that young-at-heart feeling will be all the age altering you need.

# Do You Know How to Get What You Want in Love?

How you present your needs to your partner influences the course of your romance. Discovering which of the four astrological Elements—Earth, Wind, Air, and Water—rules your relationship skills can help you build on your strengths, conquer your weaknesses, and get what you want in love!

**1** It's your birthday and your sweetie presents you with something truly hideous. How do you respond?

____ **a.** You thank him graciously and return it the next day for something you like and will actually use.

____ **b.** You're sorry that he doesn't know you well enough to give you something more appropriate, but you refuse to let him see that you're disappointed.

____ **c.** You make it clear from your dissatisfied face and body language that you're not pleased. Then you make a joke about hoping for a pony next year.

____ **d.** You coolly ask what made him choose this gift for you and insist on hearing his entire decision-making and shopping process.

**2** You were supposed to meet your man two hours ago, and he hasn't called. You react by

____ **a.** Leaving messages on his work, home, and cell phones, and checking your own messages. You figure there must be a very good reason for his tardiness.

____ **b.** Panicking. What if he was in an accident on the way over? What if he decided to leave you for that supermodel-like friend from work?

____ **c.** Seething with rage. How dare he stand you up! Even if something important came up, there's no excuse for not calling.

____ **d.** Analyzing all the reasons why he might not have showed. Were you clear about when and where you were supposed to meet? Could the two of you have miscommunicated somehow?

**3** Your honey is sexy in many ways, but his kissing technique leaves you cold. How do you let him know that you aren't satisfied?

____ **a.** You don't. You don't want to rock the boat; if you're patient enough, he'll improve with time and lots of practice.

____ **b.** You don't. Bringing up the issue isn't very romantic and could hurt his feelings; you focus instead on the passionate way he caresses and holds you.

____ **c.** The next time you're smooching, you take control of the situation, showing him exactly how you like to be kissed.

____ **d.** You tactfully say something subtle like, "Kissing you is so much fun! How about we try it this way? Wow! Wasn't that amazing?"

**4** **You're feeling bad because you just got an awful haircut. Your partner good-naturedly teases you about it, which makes you feel even worse. How do you react?**

____ **a.** You let him know that you aren't amused, but you move on because you know that it's not worth getting into a full-fledged fight over an innocent comment.

____ **b.** You burst into tears, telling him that he has really hurt your feelings. You refuse to smile until he shows some empathy.

____ **c.** You angrily walk away, slamming doors on your way out. You won't speak to him again until he does something to make up for his insensitivity.

____ **d.** You initiate a discussion about when it's okay to make light of things and when it's not. You promise to make it clear in the future when you're not in the mood for teasing.

**5** **You love holding hands and nuzzling in public, but your significant other prefers to save that behavior for private. How do you address this difference?**

____ **a.** You realize that you can't change him, and decide that as long as he shows you that he loves you in other ways, it doesn't bother you.

____ **b.** You turn to your friends for advice, worried that there's something missing in your relationship—shouldn't your lover want to show the world how he feels about you?

____ **c.** You flirtatiously grab his hand or kiss his cheek whenever you feel like it. How can he resist you when you're so alluring?

____ **d.** You understand that everyone has a different comfort level with public displays of affection, and try to find a compromise between his need for privacy and your need for physical demonstrations of love.

**6** Your partner loves rugged camping trips; your idea of "roughing it" is a low-key hotel. When he suggests a weekend in the great outdoors, you

____ **a.** Suggest that he take his outdoorsy best friend, and that the two of you go away to a place you both like the following weekend.

____ **b.** Give it a shot since it means so much to him. It could be kind of fun to snuggle under the stars.

____ **c.** Do everything in your power to convince him to take you elsewhere—you really don't want to go camping.

____ **d.** Agree to go with him if he promises to make an equal sacrifice in the future.

**7** You feel ready to take your relationship to the next level, but your partner is happy with the way things stand. How do you proceed?

____ **a.** You don't want to rush him if he isn't ready, so you set a time of how long you're willing to wait for him to commit at a higher level.

____ **b.** You can't help distancing yourself a bit. You're trying to understand, but you're deeply hurt by his refusal to move things forward.

____ **c.** You offer an ultimatum: Either he moves up to your speed or you're out the door. You don't have time to wait for him to figure things out.

____ **d.** You ask him to describe where he sees the relationship in six months, a year, and so on, to gauge where the relationship is going.

**8** When you and your partner have an argument, who is usually the first one to apologize?

____ **a.** If you started the argument, you apologize; if he started it, you let him ask for forgiveness.

____ **b.** On the brink of tears, you often apologize even if you're not wrong because you hate any bad feelings in your relationship.

____ **c.** Since your being wrong is about as likely as oceanfront property in Nebraska, he tends to cave in and apologize first.

____ **d.** Neither of you really apologizes: You usually discuss the issue until you're both feeling good about things again.

**9** Although you and your mate have a long-standing Saturday night date, you're craving some quality time with your friends this weekend. What do you do?

____ **a.** You hang out with your sweetie and make plans to catch up with your pals for Sunday brunch—you won't break your Saturday night plans without giving plenty of notice.

____ **b.** You trust your feelings and break your date: If you're really desiring some time with your friends, that probably means you've been neglecting them.

____ **c.** You plan a big group outing for Saturday night, including your partner, your friends, your partner's friends, and your friends' partners.

____ **d.** You divide your night evenly: You have dinner with your pals and go out dancing with your partner afterward.

**10** Typically, you take on all the housework, but you've been busy and now your home is a disaster. What happens next?

____ **a.** You can't stand it anymore, so you tackle the mess, but let your partner know that next time you expect more help from him.

____ **b.** You clean up the mess wordlessly, but brood if your partner doesn't give you sufficient praise and thanks afterward.

____ **c.** You stubbornly hold out: Let him deal with it for once!

____ **d.** You create a chart outlining each person's chores so this sort of disaster never happens again.

**11** Your lover's gorgeous ex keeps calling and wants to meet him for dinner. You're uncomfortable with the idea. What do you do?

____ **a.** You ask your mate about his reasons for wanting to see this person. If the explanation sounds innocent, you let him go without a major fight.

____ **b.** You become visibly upset and make it clear that the situation would make you feel jealous and insecure.

____ **c.** You lash out and let him know that there's no reason to see this person if he truly loves you. In short, you make him choose between you.

____ **d.** You encourage your mate to see the situation from another perspective: How would he feel if you met up with your sexy ex? If he's okay with the idea, then you're okay with it, too.

**⑫ Which celebrity would play you in a movie about your relationship?**

____ **a.** Gwyneth Paltrow, because she's practical and steady in her private life

____ **b.** Angelina Jolie, because she loves so passionately and intensely

____ **c.** Madonna, because she's determined to always get what she wants

____ **d.** Nicole Kidman, because she's diplomatic and thoughtful in her actions

# Scoring

Add up the number of As, Bs, Cs, and Ds you chose. Find the category in which you had the most responses to determine which astrological Element rules your relationship style and learn how to get what you want in love. Also check out the other elements that influence you to a lesser degree based on your responses.

## (Mostly As)
### Even-Tempered Earth

Because you are so practical and grounded, you can stand up for yourself when it truly matters, and you don't worry about less important relationship issues. You are a master of picking your battles, and because of this you avoid many of the petty arguments that other couples have. While being so reasonable and steady keeps you from rocking the boat, you might want to tap into your emotions a bit more. If something bothers you, it's okay to let your partner know, even if you dislike the idea of taking a risk and putting your feelings on the line. Your sweetheart is likely to feel honored that you trust him enough to share your most intimate thoughts.

## (Mostly Bs)
### Whimsical Water

Do you believe that sometimes you feel things more intensely than other people? Chances are that you do, because people who are influenced by Water tend to be especially intuitive, emotional, and sensitive. Because you wear your heart on your sleeve, your partner is able to read what you're thinking and feeling very easily, and this helps him to understand what you need. Still, sometimes you have a tendency to let your tears speak for you, and this can cause your partner to take you less seriously. You might want to surprise him every now and then by presenting clear, logical reasons for how you're feeling. He'll likely respect your thoughts and be more willing to see things from your perspective.

## (Mostly Cs)
### Fervent Fire

You know exactly what you want and how to get it! You aren't afraid to demand what you deserve, and you refuse to settle for anything less. Your mate respects your strong, brave, and energetic nature. You make it clear what you will and will not tolerate, so he always knows where he stands. Unfortunately sometimes you make what you want a little *too* clear. By always expecting someone to cater to your wants and needs, you can upset the relationship's equilibrium by putting the focus on *your* desires. Use your energy to give him what he needs every now and then. You'll see that making

sacrifices or compromises doesn't mean losing yourself.

## (Mostly Ds)
### Accommodating Air

How do you do it? Even if you're upset about something, you remain calm. You're able to see all sides of a problem and analyze and reason through the issue until both you and your mate are satisfied. You may have to concede a few points that are important to you, but you see it as a small price to pay for keeping the relationship balance intact. Although your mate values your objectivity and inventive solutions, he may not have a clear sense of what *you* really want or need. It may seem selfish to let your partner know when you need something from him, but he'll be pleased to see your true passions come to the surface.

# 3

# Improve Your Dating Life

**And make the most of your Saturday nights**

Who Is Your Ideal Mate?

Are You Right for Him?

Are You Waiting to Be Rescued by Mr. Right?

Are You a Great Date?

Are You Really Just Friends?

Is It a Summer Fling—Or the Real Thing?

Should You Dump Him?

The Post-Breakup Test: Are You Better Off without Him?

Say Goodbye to Your Ex Test: Are You Ready to Move On?

# Who Is Your Ideal Mate?

Before you can find the man of your dreams, you have to know the type of guy who will make you happy. Take this quiz to determine what qualities *your* Mr. Right must have.

**1** Your just-married girlfriend is visiting for the weekend on a mission to get you coupled off. Where do the two of you go on your "manhunt"?

____ **a.** A major league baseball game

____ **b.** A poetry reading at the local coffee house

____ **c.** Dancing at your favorite nightclub

____ **d.** A museum benefit

**2** Which of these pickup lines is most likely to work on you?

____ **a.** "How do you stay in such great shape?"

____ **b.** "Read any good books lately?"

____ **c.** "What do you do for fun?"

____ **d.** "Your place or mine?"

**3** You're on a dinner date. When the waiter comes to take your order, you hope the guy you're with

____ **a.** Has a big appetite—the portions look huge and you'll never finish yours alone

____ **b.** Asks you what you would like

____ **c.** Wants to share some of your favorite dishes

____ **d.** Orders for you, from appetizer through dessert—you get a kick out of old-fashioned, man-in-command behavior

**4** In an effort to get out and meet guys, you sign up to volunteer for a local politician's campaign. Your first day on the job, you take a look around and head straight for the

____ **a.** Door—you'll have better luck joining a coed softball league

____ **b.** Speech-writing committee

____ **c.** Event-planning committee

____ **d.** Politician himself

**5** A first-date goodnight kiss can make you say yes to seeing the guy again if it

____ **a.** Is accompanied by a fun gesture, like a high-five or bear hug

____ **b.** Is planted gingerly on your cheek, followed by a gentle squeeze of your hand

____ **c.** Is sweet and somewhat teasing and shows off his playful personality

____ **d.** Lands right on your lips—you don't want to be left wondering whether or not the guy wants to see you again

**6** You invite the new man you've been seeing to your family's house for a Sunday afternoon barbecue. If he's the kind of guy you think he is, he

____ **a.** Plants himself in front of the TV to watch football with the rest of the fans in the house

____ **b.** Brings flowers for both you and your mother

____ **c.** Offers to man the grill—he makes a mean burger

____ **d.** Effortlessly makes conversation with everyone, including your oh-so-dull brother-in-law

**7** You're at the video store looking for a flick for your date with Ben and Jerry. Suddenly you find yourself flirting with a guy who just rented

____ **a.** *Hoosiers*

____ **b.** *Sense and Sensibility*

____ **c.** *There's Something about Mary*

____ **d.** *The Firm*

**8** When the guy you've been seeing asks you to be his date for a wedding, you look at this as

____ **a.** A challenge to see if you can keep up with him on the dance floor

____ **b.** A gesture that he wants a commitment but is too scared to show it

____ **c.** An opportunity to meet and party with his friends

____ **d.** A sign he knows you're the one

**9** At work you're most likely to take notice of a male coworker in

____ **a.** The Nerf basketball area

____ **b.** The library

____ **c.** A huddle of laughing coworkers

____ **d.** The executive dining room

**⑩** If your life were being made into a made-for-TV movie, you would want your leading man to be a

_____ **a.** Michael Jordan type

_____ **b.** Joseph Fiennes type

_____ **c.** Jim Carrey type

_____ **d.** George Stephanopoulos type

# Scoring

Add up the number of As, Bs, Cs, and Ds you chose. Find the category in which you had the most responses to determine your ideal mate. Also check out what other types of guys may be right for you, based on your next highest number of responses.

### (Mostly As)
## The Sporty Stud

In your arena jock-like guys are number one. You favor a man who likes football over one who brings flowers. Why? For starters, you're attracted to a competitive spirit and the drive to win. Not to mention that a guy who loves the game is probably pretty playful. Translated into a relationship, these qualities can be top-notch, although the same qualities that initially attract you may also drive you crazy at times.

A competitive guy may make a terrific athlete, but that same quality may make him feel like he's competing for your feelings—with your friends, your family, your job, and so on. Likewise, _you_ may sometimes feel like you're competing with _his_ friends, athletic hobbies, and so on. But this type of man considers himself a team player, so in a relationship you'll be able to count on him to be supportive, interested in your opinions, and willing to work together to make the two of you a winning pair.

### (Mostly Bs)
## The Sensitive Guy

Isn't he sweet? You definitely go for the guy who has a serious case of feelings—whether he wears them on his sleeve or not. Manners seem important to him, and to you. And it's a good bet your soul mate would as easily tune in to ballads on the radio as stage a protest against cruelty to animals. Tapping into his soft side, however, may not always be so easy. A guy who's clued in to his feelings may also be protective of them. So if you find yourself face-to-face with one of these sweeties, don't wait for him to make the first move. Let him know you want to get to know him better. Sensitive types think with their brain as well as their heart—he'll get the hint.

## (Mostly Cs)
## The Fun-Loving Fellow

Whether at a gathering with friends or in line at a movie, you pick out the most personable guy of the group, and it's easy to see why: You enjoy a good time and a good laugh, and need someone who can appreciate these as much as you do. A man like this can hold his own in any situation and with anybody. But he is not necessarily discerning: He may as easily chat up your grandmother as his beautiful next-door neighbor. But don't consider his charming nature his fatal flaw; remember it's what drew you to him in the first place. But do keep in mind that his "playfulness" may make it tough for him to settle down.

## (Mostly Ds)
## The Confident Chap

You definitely know what you want—a guy who's sure of himself. This self-assuredness has gotten him where he wants to be: possibly at the top of the corporate ladder, the president of his condo board, or the most sought-after when his friends need advice. What you gain is a companion who knows most of the answers and will make you feel safe and cared for. As great as this type of support can be, the reality is that your ideas and his won't always mesh. And once you tell him your take on a situation, he may argue and try to get you to see things his way. Don't let this get you down or make you stop thinking for yourself. As long as you don't let his strong personality overpower you or take away your independence, you and Mr. Confident can make quite a pair. After all, a difference in opinions makes any relationship more interesting.

# Are You Right for Him?

Besides thinking about what kind of guy is Mr. Right for you, you also have to consider if you're Ms. Right for him. That depends a lot on how your character traits match up with his. Answer these questions to discover your true personality based on how the four astrological Elements (Fire, Water, Earth, Air) influence you, and find out what kind of man will have stars in his eyes for you.

**1** **Choose the following group of words that most closely describes you:**

___ **a.** Impatient, energetic, brave, spontaneous

___ **b.** Grounded, sensual, stubborn, practical

___ **c.** Intellectual, a good communicator, witty, always thinking

___ **d.** Emotional, artistic, moody, a dreamer

**2** **Which of the following statements best describes your attitude toward work?**

___ **a.** You like to be the head of the team. It doesn't matter if you have the expertise or not—you just pretend you do! That's why delegating is your key strategy.

___ **b.** Sometimes it's difficult to get yourself going on a new project, but once you do, you're quite an efficient worker. Your boss loves your attention to detail and dedication to your work.

___ **c.** Work is okay as long as it's fun, inspiring, varied—and as long as you have plenty of cute coworkers to flirt with to make the day pass more quickly!

___ **d.** At work you tend to take on the role of confidante—people come to you with their coworker gripes, their complaints about the boss, and their extra work. You tend to get a lot dumped onto you.

**3** **When a friend invites you to take a day off work so you can enjoy a luxurious day at the spa, how do you respond?**

___ **a.** "Oooh, heck, yeah—count me in! It's your treat, right?"

___ **b.** "Oh, I don't know what to do—I could really, really use a massage and a facial, but I have so much work to do."

___ **c.** "Sure, sounds great, and maybe after we hit the spa we can top off the day with a movie."

___ **d.** "Well, okay, but maybe instead of spending all that money at the spa, we could go out to the natural hot springs."

**4** **When you decide to ignore your errands on a Saturday and do whatever you want, how do you spend your day?**

___ **a.** At the amusement park, eating hot dogs and riding the roller coaster until you're nearly sick.

___ **b.** Shopping at the newest, hippest boutiques—if you can't spend any money, you can at least window shop and try on clothes.

___ **c.** At a poetry slam at the hip coffee shop downtown—you love teasing the performers, checking out the artsy decor, and chatting up all the coffee shop hunks.

___ **d.** At home, curled up in bed with a novel and your cat at your feet.

**5** **What kind of gift do you most love to receive?**

___ **a.** Something fun that you can use

___ **b.** Something classy and expensive

___ **c.** Something unique, different, and unusual

___ **d.** Something sentimental, especially something homemade

**6** **How do you feel about arguments with people who are close to you?**

___ **a.** You're pretty used to them by now—they happen pretty often.

___ **b.** You don't like them, but you always want to represent your view of things, which sometimes leads to arguments.

___ **c.** You like arguments—you consider them the perfect forum for your debating skills.

___ **d.** You hate arguments—you don't like any discord between you and your loved ones.

**7** **What were your parents like when you were growing up?**

____ **a.** Generally easy-going and fun, but there was some arguing between you and them

____ **b.** Stern disciplinarians, but very loving

____ **c.** Intellectuals—somewhat emotionally aloof but always interesting

____ **d.** Very loving, kind, and connected—sometimes too emotionally connected

**8** **How do you feel about pets?**

____ **a.** You like them fine, but you don't think you would be a very good pet owner—you're hardly ever home and you tend to forget things (like feeding times and walks).

____ **b.** You like dogs—they have so much personality and provide such steady, high-quality companionship.

____ **c.** You like interesting, beautiful pets that don't require much intense interaction and care—exotic birds, fish, and rare reptiles are just your speed.

____ **d.** You love all pets. You feel like you communicate with them on a deep level and believe that all animals have souls and feelings.

**9** **What about yourself would you most like to work on or change?**

____ **a.** Sometimes you're a little too reckless; you wish you could learn to slow down and be patient.

____ **b.** At times you can be somewhat stubborn or narrow-minded; you need to learn how to cope better with change and chaos.

____ **c.** You tend to be a bit flaky or flighty; you wish you could develop better focus.

____ **d.** You're such a dreamer; you wish you could be a little more grounded in the here and now.

**10** **What do you feel are the best traits that you have to offer a friend or a lover?**

____ **a.** You're a lot of fun and always up for a good time.

____ **b.** You're very sensible and practical, so you give good advice and provide a good example.

____ **c.** You're a quick thinker, and you're especially attuned to art and literature.

____ **d.** You're a good listener, and you really care about other people and their feelings.

# Scoring

Add up the number of As, Bs, Cs, and Ds you chose. Find the category in which you had the most responses to determine which Element rules your personality most—and discover what type of man desires you. Also check out the other Elements that influence your personality—and the men you attract—based on your responses.

### (Mostly As)
## You Are Ruled by Fire

You've got lots of Fire energy motivating your actions and desires and may have some Fire in your birth chart. If the man of your dreams is a Fire Sign—Aries, Leo, or Sagittarius—your connection will be truly hot and a lot of fun. However, your relationship could turn out to be dangerously combustible, so be careful. If your man is an Air Sign—Gemini, Libra, or Aquarius—that's also a good match, because Air fuels Fire and helps it spread, and Fire Signs always keep Air Signs interested and guessing. If your man is an Earth or a Water Sign, yours may be a less than perfectly smooth and flowing relationship. If he's a Taurus, Virgo, or Capricorn, your heady energy and risky behavior might put him on edge. And if he's a Cancer, Scorpio, or Pisces, you might be a bit too insensitive for him—though he's so sensitive himself, he probably won't say anything about it.

### (Mostly Bs)
## You Are Ruled by Earth

You approach life in an Earthy way—you're grounded, sensual, practical, and reliable. Perhaps you have some Earth Signs in your birth chart. If your Mr. Right is an Earth Sign—a Taurus, Virgo, or Capricorn—he's probably attracted to you for your dependability and loyalty, not to mention your utter sensuality. The Water Signs—Cancer, Scorpio, and Pisces—also make great matches for Earth Signs. If your man is a Water Sign, he's a bit of an emotional dreamer who appreciates the firm, steady base you provide him. If your man is a Fire or an Air Sign, yours might be a case of opposites attracting. If he's an Aries, Leo, or Sagittarius, don't be surprised if he finds your relaxed, sensual nature a bit too . . . well, relaxed. And if he's a Gemini, Libra, or Aquarius, he might be interested in something other than your witty repartee.

(Mostly Cs)

## You Are Ruled by Air

You've got the markings of an Air Sign—Gemini, Libra or Aquarius. You may have some Air in your birth chart, as you tend to approach things from an intellectual point of view and can't stay attracted to someone who doesn't stimulate you mentally, first and foremost. The man who falls for you also may be an Air Sign, as yours would truly be a meeting of the minds (and wits). If he's a Fire Sign—Aries, Leo, or Sagittarius—he might not be as into art and literature as you are, but he's still likely to appreciate your scintillating wit and fun social nature. If he's an Earth or a Water Sign, you two might be meeting on some other level. If he's a Taurus, Virgo, or Capricorn, he may love your mind, but wish it were a bit more focused or dedicated. And if he's a Cancer, Scorpio, or Pisces, he might try to get you to spend more time at home with him, sharing your thoughts and feelings.

(Mostly Ds)

## You Are Ruled by Water

You may feel Water's influence in your birth chart, as you certainly feel it in your daily life—you're sensitive, emotional, and deep, possessed of a poetic and romantic nature. If your man is a Water Sign as well—Cancer, Scorpio, or Pisces—you're probably a great match, as you share an intuitive connection and both have compassionate, understanding natures. If he's an Earth Sign—Taurus, Virgo, or Capricorn—he loves you for your deeply emotional nature, and loves to provide you with the grounding influence you need. If he's a Fire or an Air Sign, yours may not have been the most natural or immediate of connections—which isn't to say it can't work between you. If he's an Aries, Leo, or Sagittarius, he might find you a bit too clingy and sensitive. And if he's a Gemini, Libra, or Aquarius, he might be put off or intimidated by the emotional way you approach the world.

# Are You Waiting to Be Rescued by Mr. Right?

Sure, you tell your mother, nosy coworkers, and your favorite fitness instructor that you're just fine being alone. But are you enjoying every *single* day? Answer these questions and find out if you're making the most of your single status—or wasting your days waiting for Mr. Wonderful (without even knowing it!).

**1** **In what style is your home furnished?**

____ **a.** Your place is part Ikea/part hand-me-downs from the folks—it doesn't feel entirely comfortable, but it'll do for now.

____ **b.** Your home could be pictured on the pages of an interior design magazine.

____ **c.** Furnished? Oh, you mean other than boxes and beanbags? Won't I have plenty of time (and money) for that kind of homey stuff when I'm married?

**2** **Your boss offers you a promotion with a raise and more responsibility. You**

____ **a.** Accept, but with a little trepidation—what if your next date is the type who is threatened by a successful woman?

____ **b.** Turn it down—extra hours would cut down on time spent mingling and man hunting

____ **c.** Accept, do a little victory dance, and treat yourself to a shopping spree

**3** **It's your birthday, with no man in the picture. Your plans are**

____ **a.** A quiet night on your own—celebrating milestones with girlfriends is nice, but a little depressing

____ **b.** A quiet dinner with your close chick friends—it'll be fun, but it would be even better if you had a date

____ **c.** The best possible plans a gal could have—you're throwing yourself a small dinner party with close friends and family

**4** You've been invited to be in your best friend's bridal party. As her big day draws near, what do you honestly feel?

____ **a.** Joy, for her as well as for your-self—both of you are where you want to be in your lives.

____ **b.** Happiness mixed with wistful-ness—she deserves the best, but if life were truly fair you'd be getting hitched as well.

____ **c.** Pure, unadulterated envy—when, oh when, will it be your turn?

**5** You've accrued a week's vacation time. You decide to

____ **a.** Stay home—solo vacations just aren't fun, and this way you'll have a chance to relax and catch up on sleep and chores

____ **b.** Enroll in an intensive work-shop—you've always dreamed of having time to focus on your favorite hobby

____ **c.** Go on a tropical vacation—you like the beach but are a little worried that it may turn out to be a real bore on your own

**6** You're on a blind date that is going well. You

____ **a.** Decide the evening is more proof that life is full of pleasant surprises

____ **b.** Wonder when he'll call to ask you on a second date and a third and a . . .

____ **c.** Try not to get your hopes up but can imagine telling your friends, "I think I met the one"

**7** You arrive at a friend's dinner party only to discover that you're the sole single person. Your reaction is

____ **a.** To make the best of it—maybe someone there knows a great single guy

____ **b.** To enjoy the good food and stimu-lating conversation

____ **c.** To invent a bad headache and split—you could find a million other things to do that would be way more fun

**8** Someone you've been dating for two weeks suddenly displays a possessive streak when another man looks at you. What is your reaction?

____ **a.** You wish he was more easygoing, but you're not about to let something so small get in the way of a potentially great relationship.

___ **b.** You tell him there is no cause for jealousy and decide that if he acts inappropriately again you'll reevaluate the relationship.

___ **c.** You break things off—this guy's got a bad disposition, and you just can't be bothered with it.

**9** **For months you've been walking around feeling blue. You**

___ **a.** Figure you'll feel better when your luck changes in the love department

___ **b.** Consider going to therapy and determining the root of the problem

___ **c.** Go on a vacation—a change of scenery always does wonders for the blues, and maybe you'll meet someone interesting

**10** **At a family gathering your nosy aunt asks if there's a wedding in your future. You**

___ **a.** Laugh and respond, "Sorry, I'm still single and loving it."

___ **b.** Get defensive and say, "I'm still single, which suits me but obviously not you. Sorry to be a disappointment."

___ **c.** Lie and say you're seeing someone seriously—you don't need her bugging you.

# Scoring

Give yourself the numerical value that matches each of your answers. Then add all 10 scores together and use your total score to find your result category.

1. a – 2  b – 1  c – 3
2. a – 2  b – 3  c – 1
3. a – 3  b – 2  c – 1
4. a – 1  b – 2  c – 3
5. a – 3  b – 1  c – 2
6. a – 1  b – 3  c – 2
7. a – 2  b – 1  c – 3
8. a – 3  b – 2  c – 1
9. a – 3  b – 1  c – 2
10. a – 1  b – 2  c – 3

(24–30 points)
## Waiting for Mr. Wonderful

You're cheating yourself of many of life's pleasures by thinking of yourself as incomplete without a man. Even though the idea of a big white dress is hard to resist, desperation to wed can lead to unwise choices in love partners, not to mention a less-than-satisfying life. You may need some time to refuel and get to know (and love) yourself. Call a dating moratorium while you devote time to self-nurturing activities:

spend time with close friends, take up new hobbies, rededicate yourself to your job, fix up your apartment. You also might consider meditation—there is nothing like getting in touch with the fabulous inner you to quiet those "I'm nothing without a man" blues. The bonus: The happier and more fulfilled you are on your own, the more likely you are to attract a like-minded person who can become not your rescuer, but your partner.

## (17–23 points)
## A Knight Would Be Nice

You have created a mostly satisfying life, full of friends, fun, and accomplishment. But you derail yourself by succumbing to periods of intense longing for that mythical guy in shining armor. Don't put off making all areas of your life as satisfying as possible. For example, having a home that feels like a haven (not a temporary pit stop) adds to your emotional wellness. It's also a good idea to regularly remind yourself of your accomplishments and blessings in life. Counteract those occasional "I don't have a man in my life" blues with

self-affirming mantras. Look in the mirror every morning and say, "I have a full, happy life, whether I am with a man or not." You'll be amazed at how good a repeated phrase like that can make you feel. The bonus: Revel in your strength, and strong men will be attracted to you.

## (10–16 points)
## Not Looking for a Rescuer, Thanks

You are blessed with the capacity to thoroughly enjoy your life and the people in it. No doubt you have a purposeful existence, terrific living space, and a great job. You go on vacations to get away from it all—not as an excuse to hunt for men. And, best of all, you feel no need to apologize to anyone because you don't have a man on your arm. One caveat: If you do want to settle down eventually, be careful not to get so comfortable in your single lifestyle that you are unable to recognize a potential Mr. Right when he crosses the horizon. Given your outlook, you're sure to find a man who's as self-confident and comfortable in his own skin as you are. You two will make a great team!

# Are You a Great Date?

Attracting a good guy is one small step on the long road to commitment. To have date number one lead to number two and beyond, you must be adept in the art of dating. Are your dating skills helping or hurting your romantic chances? Take this quiz and find out if you could be sabotaging your love life.

**1** **When a close friend offers to set you up with a guy she knows, you tell her you'll go as long as**

____ **a.** He's a nice guy

____ **b.** He's good-looking

____ **c.** She does all of your grocery shopping for a year

**2** **You wear your favorite first-date outfit only to learn (thanks to his half-joking comment) that he doesn't like your attire. You**

____ **a.** Vow not to go out with him again—if he doesn't like your look, he's not for you

____ **b.** Make a mental note for next time so you can wear something he likes

____ **c.** Toss back a teasing dis of your own and forget about his comment

**3** **You suspect that a man you're becoming intimate with is seeing other women. Although you two aren't exclusive, you want to know whether he's sharing his popcorn/TV/bed with someone else. What do you do?**

____ **a.** Ask him.

____ **b.** Casually mention the other (imaginary) men you're seeing and see whether he takes the bait and spills his story.

____ **c.** Nothing—at this point in your relationship, it's none of your business.

**4** **Your closest female friend has started dating someone, and it looks serious. As a result, you**

____ **a.** Are depressed—why can't that happen to you?

____ **b.** Are a bit peeved—she never spends any time with you anymore

____ **c.** Are genuinely happy for her—if it can happen for her, it can happen for you

**5** Your date mentions that he and his buddies like to play paintball. You

____ **a.** Ask him what he likes about it

____ **b.** Ask if you can go along

____ **c.** Tell him how opposed you are to acts of violence

**6** Five days, eight hours, and twenty-three minutes ago, you went out with a new guy and had a great time. He hasn't called yet, so you decide to do the calling. When he answers, you

____ **a.** Wimp out and hang up—hopefully he won't know it was you

____ **b.** Tell him you were just wondering why he hasn't called you

____ **c.** Tell him you just wanted to call to say what a great time you had

**7** Your Saturday nights are looking a bit too empty for comfort. What do you do to try to kill the loneliness blues?

____ **a.** Tell a few carefully selected people—none of whom belong to the same social circle—that you're ready to be fixed up

____ **b.** Resolve to leave the next party you attend with at least two men's phone numbers

____ **c.** Go on the Internet and enter a singles chat room you've never been in before

**8** You can't help noticing the adorable guy who takes the same train you do almost every night. The next time you find yourself standing on the train platform with him, you

____ **a.** Wait for him to board the train first, so you can sit near him

____ **b.** Wait for him to board the train first, so you can sit next to him

____ **c.** Wait for him to board the train first, so you can sit in a different car—if he's interested, he'll come find you

**9** Having recently ended a serious relationship, you naturally find yourself thinking of your ex sometimes. He enters your thoughts most often when

____ **a.** You're sifting through the many mementos—concert tickets, vacation photos, love notes—from your relationship

____ **b.** You meet a new guy—you can't help comparing and contrasting them

____ **c.** You're getting ready to go out with a new guy—if your ex could see you, he'd be so sorry

**10** A coworker asks whether you want to go with her to a social event at a rock-climbing gym. Extreme sports are not exactly your forte. What do you tell her?

____ **a.** "Sure, I'd love to go."

____ **b.** "I'm afraid of heights. But thanks anyway."

____ **c.** "I can't make it that night, but how about we go out after work next Wednesday?"

**11** You meet a man (in a bar, a chat room, wherever), and the two of you hit it off. By the end of the night, he knows

____ **a.** Your name

____ **b.** Your three favorite jokes, how fast you can run a mile, and the fact that, given your skills, you deserve a raise at work

____ **c.** What you do for a living, that you love to salsa dance, and your email address

**12** Your date mentions that he loves to go spelunking. You have no idea what he's talking about, so you

____ **a.** Say, "Really? Me, too!"

____ **b.** Say, "What's spelunking?"

____ **c.** Change the topic

**13** When a date calls to ask what you want to do when you two go out, you usually

____ **a.** Say you don't care—because, honestly, you really don't

____ **b.** Suggest seeing a movie—it's the most painless dating experience you can think of

____ **c.** Mention an activity you enjoy, like hiking, bowling, or going to a museum—anything that will let you both relax and have some fun

**14** At a wedding, a guy who is really not your type asks you to dance. You

____ **a.** Say yes—he might seem like a better catch once you get to know him

____ **b.** Say yes—no one else will probably ask, so why not?

____ **c.** Say no—you don't want to waste your time dancing with him when there are so many other single guys in the room

**15** After weeks of emailing each other, you and Mr. Could-Be-Right have decided to meet face to face, and your nerves are shot. Why?

____ **a.** You're worried that you won't like him in person.

___ **b.** You two are so compatible online, you're worried about ruining a great relationship.

___ **c.** You sent him a photograph taken when you were much thinner and younger.

# Scoring

Give yourself the numerical value that matches each of your answers. Then add all 15 scores together and use your total score to find your result category.

1. **a** – 3  **b** – 2  **c** – 1
2. **a** – 1  **b** – 2  **c** – 3
3. **a** – 3  **b** – 2  **c** – 1
4. **a** – 1  **b** – 2  **c** – 3
5. **a** – 2  **b** – 3  **c** – 1
6. **a** – 2  **b** – 1  **c** – 3
7. **a** – 3  **b** – 2  **c** – 1
8. **a** – 2  **b** – 3  **c** – 1
9. **a** – 1  **b** – 2  **c** – 3
10. **a** – 3  **b** – 1  **c** – 2
11. **a** – 1  **b** – 2  **c** – 3
12. **a** – 2  **b** – 3  **c** – 1
13. **a** – 1  **b** – 2  **c** – 3
14. **a** – 3  **b** – 1  **c** – 2
15. **a** – 2  **b** – 3  **c** – 1

(35–45 points)
## Dream Date

Your social calendar should be booked solid. When it comes to dating, you know how important it is to go out, be seen, and give off a positive attitude, all of which help draw guys to you. Not to mention your confidence and take-action attitude, which not only attract men but make you feel good too. When you're on a date, you're careful to offer just enough information about yourself to keep him interested without spilling your life story (that can come later), and you show plenty of interest in his life without acting like a love-struck groupie. But it's clear from your confident approach to dating that your life does not revolve around men. You know how important it is to spend time with friends and to pursue your own interests and hobbies. If attending a lecture by your favorite writer or taking your favorite exercise class just happens to result in your meeting a new man, all the better. No doubt you do all this for your own happiness—but it also makes you a better catch!

(25–34 points)

## First-Date Queen

You're not bad at getting first dates; it's those second dates that often seem elusive. Could be because you're too busy playing dating games or putting on an act to make a true impression. Instead of working so hard to spark stimulating conversation or make him feel like Mr. Wonderful, try acting more natural. Once you start playing games you'll be stuck playing them, and you'll miss the opportunity to really get to know your date and to let him really get to know you. Provide good, honest information (but no need to mention your ex, your work woes, or your mother's desperate attempts to get you married). If it's clear that you've both enjoyed the first date, don't wait for him to call you to ask for a second; call him (but never hang up without saying something!). That take-charge suggestion also goes for asking him out, or at least supplying your phone number. Making the first move shows men you're confident, a quality that worthwhile guys like in a woman.

(15–24 points)

## Downer Date

Hate to say it, but you could use a class in Dating 101. And the first lesson is how to have a more positive attitude. Excluding those few dud dates (and, face it, everyone experiences some), dating is supposed to be fun. If nothing else, it's an opportunity to try out a new restaurant, wear a new outfit, or go to a movie you've been dying to see. No one's asking you to plaster on a fake happy face or to act unnatural, but try to show some enthusiasm. And maybe even practice making the first (or second or third) move once in a while. You have nothing to lose and, yes, everything to gain. Think of it this way: If someone who hardly knows you rebuffs you, it's certainly not a negative statement about you as a person. But being optimistic and open to intimacy is one thing; being desperate and needy is another. Besides scaring guys away (fast!), neediness blinds you to what a guy is really all about and saps your self-confidence. And more than anything else, you need to be happy with yourself to be a great date.

# Are You Really Just Friends?

You and a certain male someone are spending scads of time together, but how can you tell if all of this closeness is leading anywhere romantic? Answer these questions and find out if your friendship is purely platonic—or soon to be something more.

**1** **How often do you see each other?**

____ **a.** About once a week

____ **b.** Every day

____ **c.** Only occasionally

**2** **Have you met your male friend's friends?**

____ **a.** No, you hardly even know who they are.

____ **b.** Yes, but only because you've run into them on occasion.

____ **c.** Yes, he made it a point to introduce you to them.

**3** **If he has a serious problem at work or in some other aspect of his life, you're likely to find out about it by**

____ **a.** His confiding the details and asking your advice

____ **b.** Accidentally overhearing him discuss his woes with someone else

____ **c.** Mental telepathy—he has his "all's right with the world" face on when you're together

**4** **Does "the future" ever come up in conversation?**

____ **a.** Well, he bought you tickets to a baseball game that's a month away.

____ **b.** Yes—he talks about where you will spend next summer together.

____ **c.** Hmm, now that you think of it, not really—you hardly even discuss the coming weekend.

**5** **If you ask him to do a favor for you, he is**

____ **a.** Johnny on the spot

____ **b.** The man with good intentions but a thousand excuses

____ **c.** Mr. Invisible

**6** His romantic history shows him to be the type who

____ **a.** Has loved—and left—quite a few

____ **b.** Can easily make a commitment

____ **c.** Hasn't shut the door on marriage but is scarred by past failures

**7** The longer you know each other

____ **a.** The more you realize that there is a lot to learn about what makes him tick

____ **b.** The more frustrating it becomes that you still feel like casual buddies

____ **c.** The better you know each other and the closer you become

**8** Whenever you dial his cell phone

____ **a.** He answers immediately

____ **b.** He calls you back within a few hours

____ **c.** He calls back just as you're about to file a missing-person report

**9** If your birthday were today, what type of present would you most likely get from him?

____ **a.** Jewelry

____ **b.** A funny e-card

____ **c.** A CD

**10** Do you feel secure that you're the only woman in his life?

____ **a.** Absolutely—he doesn't even seem to look at other women!

____ **b.** Definitely . . . well, almost definitely—he doesn't talk about other women, but sometimes you get the sense they're around.

____ **c.** Unfortunately not—in fact, you feel pretty sure that you're not the only woman in his life.

## Scoring

Give yourself the numerical value that matches each of your answers. Then add all 10 scores together and use your total score to find your result category.

1. **a** – 2  **b** – 3  **c** – 1
2. **a** – 1  **b** – 2  **c** – 3
3. **a** – 3  **b** – 2  **c** – 1
4. **a** – 2  **b** – 3  **c** – 1
5. **a** – 3  **b** – 2  **c** – 1
6. **a** – 1  **b** – 3  **c** – 2
7. **a** – 2  **b** – 1  **c** – 3
8. **a** – 3  **b** – 2  **c** – 1
9. **a** – 3  **b** – 1  **c** – 2
10. **a** – 3  **b** – 2  **c** – 1

(24–30 points)
## Sally, Have You Met Harry?

It sounds like your friendship has overtones of romance à la Billy Crystal and Meg Ryan in *When Harry Met Sally*. You've grown close, and the two of you spend a lot of time together, sharing problems as well as joys. He's introduced you to the people in his life, and let's face it, nothing spells romantic interest better than talk of future summers together, immediate cell phone pickup, and jewelry. If he hasn't yet made the first move, invite him over for dinner and a video (*When Harry Met Sally* may be too obvious!). Have *vino* on the menu and wear something special (yes, even sexy). Kick off your shoes and cuddle close when the opening credits start. One thing should lead to another.

(17–23 points)
## Passionate Pals

The guy is obviously into you, but just how deeply is open to question. He returns your calls, but you can't set your clock by the reliability of his response. He gives you presents on special occasions, but of the noncommittal sort (nothing you can wear on your neck or finger). If his friends pop up, he won't run and hide, but he's not looking to integrate you into his life. If you really want more from this guy, it's time for a talk. In a nonthreatening way, broach the subject of where he sees the relationship going. Does he think it has the potential to get serious down the road, or does he see you as a good-time Charlotte? It's better to know how things stand than to hang on to false hope. The bottom line: Take care of yourself by asking the hard questions now. Even though it's a scary thing to do, you'll save yourself time (not to mention heartache) by dealing with this sooner, rather than later.

(10–16 points)
## Fair-Weather Friend

It's time to get out your glasses (not the rose-tinted ones) and give this friendship a good looking-over. Not only is your guy not a smart romantic option, he's not such a terrific friend. He seems evasive and sometimes unreliable—not the person to list as an "emergency contact," and not the man to open your heart to. He obviously isn't ready or able to invite you into his life in a deep way, so follow his lead.

Don't make more out of this friendship than there is. Rather than opening your heart in hopes he'll reciprocate, play it cool. Try to think of him as akin to a chick buddy but with a protruding Adam's apple (not to mention other important parts). But if being around him is painful to you, then start looking for other guys (and girls) to hang out with, preferably ones who have more to give.

# Is It a Summer Fling—Or the Real Thing?

Under the influence of "summer fever," even the most no-non-sense woman may find herself strolling the sand arm-in-arm with a tanned Adonis or chatting up a friendly stranger at a sunny outdoor festival. Can a bond that starts around a bonfire grow into a real-world relationship? Find out if *your* summer love could last through Labor Day—and beyond.

**1** **When you first saw him, you thought**

____ **a.** "He looks like he's having fun."

____ **b.** "Cute/handsome/hot."

____ **c.** "I'm in love."

**2** **His opening line to you was**

____ **a.** "There's a party (or festival or event) tonight—would you like to come?"

____ **b.** "Can I buy you a piña colada, beautiful?"

____ **c.** "Where have you been all my life?"

**3** **Within a few minutes of talking to each other, you felt**

____ **a.** As if you'd known each other for years

____ **b.** Surprised at yourself: You couldn't believe you were flirting with a stranger

____ **c.** Intrigued to learn more about him

**4** **By the end of your first day together, you knew**

____ **a.** His most embarrassing moment, his birthday, his mother's name, and his hopes for the future

____ **b.** His job and his best friend's name

____ **c.** His plans for a cross-country road trip later that summer

**5** **When buying a new bathing suit during the summer, you**

____ **a.** Shop around for the most flattering and comfortable style you can find

____ **b.** Take into consideration his favorite color

____ **c.** Go for an over-the-top sexy number—you only live once!

**6** When he helps you apply sunscreen, he

____ **a.** Slaps it on without much thought

____ **b.** Is careful to get every spot so you don't burn

____ **c.** Pays particular attention to your most erogenous areas

**7** Which of the following guys are you most likely to be attracted to on vacation?

____ **a.** The sports-minded guy with the tan and the muscles

____ **b.** The good-looking, outgoing flirt

____ **c.** The soulful-looking guy walking the beach alone at night

**8** If your summer romance had a Beach Boys theme song, it would be

____ **a.** "Wouldn't It Be Nice": You could be married, and then you'd be happy, oh wouldn't it be nice?

____ **b.** "Fun Fun Fun": Till your daddy takes the T-bird away

____ **c.** "Barbara Ann": You saw him and you thought you'd take a chance

**9** By the end of the summer, you plan to get him to give you

____ **a.** The soft sweatshirt he wears every night

____ **b.** His phone number and email address

____ **c.** A promise to visit as soon as he can

**10** If September comes and you and your summer love aren't together, how will you feel?

____ **a.** Nostalgic but happy—it couldn't last, but it was wonderful.

____ **b.** Disappointed, but you know better than to take a summer romance seriously.

____ **c.** Heartbroken—you really thought the two of you were right together.

## Scoring

Give yourself the numerical value that matches each of your answers. Then add all 10 scores together and use your total score to find your result category.

1. **a** – 1  **b** – 2  **c** – 3
2. **a** – 1  **b** – 2  **c** – 3
3. **a** – 3  **b** – 1  **c** – 2
4. **a** – 3  **b** – 2  **c** – 1
5. **a** – 2  **b** – 3  **c** – 1
6. **a** – 1  **b** – 3  **c** – 2
7. **a** – 1  **b** – 2  **c** – 3
8. **a** – 3  **b** – 1  **c** – 2
9. **a** – 1  **b** – 2  **c** – 3
10. **a** – 1  **b** – 2  **c** – 3

(24–30 points)
## Something More

Oh, those summer nights! The romantic in you could never have a summer "fling" without wishing it could turn into something more. Chances are it will, as your desire for a long-lasting relationship that lasts from season to season inspires you to choose the object of your summer lovin' carefully—overlooking any guy whose most winning quality is his beach volleyball serve. You want someone you can admire in his business suit as well as in his bathing suit. More importantly, you want someone you can connect with long after Labor Day. Just remember that summer flings don't always ease into fall so easily. Remember Danny and Sandy in *Grease?* They had a lot of thorny moments trying to move their beach-based bond into the real world. In the end, they made it work, and so can you.

(17–23 points)
## Could Be Something

You're not someone who *purposefully* looks for a summer-only fling, but you wouldn't say no to a little vacation romance either. The tanned muscle men on the beach with bikini-clad babes on their mind may not inspire you to couple up, but a good-looking guy with some smooth talk and time to focus on you may just win you over for a few weeks. And, because you picked your man wisely, don't be surprised if those few weeks extend into September. Love can be mysterious—who's to say that a relationship inspired by sunsets and beach strolls can't pick up real steam and roll right into the fall? You're realistic enough to know that the chances of long-term success are slim, which helps protect your heart and your head from potential pain.

(10–16 points)

## Summer Fling

You're out for a playful good time—just some laughs and some fun in the sun, nothing too serious. You'd be amazed—and even troubled—if your summer fling dragged on into fall. You doubt if Mr. Right-for-the-Summer would be such a catch in your normal world. What would the two of you talk about? What would he think of your friends? What would you think of his? The list goes on. Make your intentions clear with him right from the start—yours isn't the only heart that needs protection. Come fall, you can cast your reel in your real world sea for a new catch.

# Should You Dump Him?

It's not always easy to know when a guy is just not right for you (ever heard the phrase "blinded by love"?). Take this test and find out whether you really belong in your current relationship—or whether you're better off bidding your beau *adieu.*

**1** **When your man is around your friends, he**

____ **a.** Acts friendly but you can tell he's not really having a great time

____ **b.** Barely disguises his desire to be elsewhere

____ **c.** Makes an honest effort to get to know them

**2** **Does your guy know your life goals and deepest desires?**

____ **a.** Of course—you two talk about your hopes and dreams with each other.

____ **b.** Somewhat—he doesn't ask about that stuff, but you've brought it up a few times.

____ **c.** No—he hasn't asked about it, so you don't feel comfortable bringing it up.

**3** **When you tell your guy that you've had a hard day at work, he**

____ **a.** Says he bets his day was worse

____ **b.** Asks what he can do to make you feel better

____ **c.** Says that's too bad or that he's sorry to hear it

**4** **When your boyfriend takes you out, he is quick to**

____ **a.** Take care of the bill

____ **b.** Take care of his half of the bill

____ **c.** Let you take care of the bill

**5** **When you broach the topic of your man meeting your family, his response is**

____ **a.** "Do I have to?"

____ **b.** "Sure, whatever you want."

____ **c.** "I can't wait."

**6** **When you get dressed up for an evening out, your guy**

____ **a.** Says how nice you look in that outfit

____ **b.** Rarely comments on how you look

____ **c.** Tells you how beautiful you are

**7** **If your man had to order dinner for you at a restaurant, would he pick the right meal for you?**

____ **a.** Of course—he knows your likes and dislikes.

____ **b.** Maybe—you're pretty sure he knows your favorite food, but if it's not on the menu, he might not know what else to order.

____ **c.** No way—you doubt he knows your likes and dislikes.

**8** **When you're not in the mood to have sex and your guy is, he**

____ **a.** Asks (sweetly) for a rain check

____ **b.** Asks (sweetly) a few more times, hoping you'll change your mind

____ **c.** Asks (not so sweetly) why you're never in the mood

**9** **When you want to talk about how you're feeling or what you're thinking, he**

____ **a.** Is willing to listen only after you practically beg him

____ **b.** Is usually willing to drop what he's doing to listen

____ **c.** Is willing to listen as long as he's not in the middle of something (like watching a game on TV)

**10** **If you wanted to do something to improve your relationship, he would**

____ **a.** Ask why your relationship needs improving

____ **b.** Probably go along with whatever it is

____ **c.** Tell you that your relationship doesn't need any improving

**11** **When you're in the mood for a stimulating conversation, you turn to**

____ **a.** Your guy

____ **b.** Your guy if your best friend isn't around

____ **c.** Anyone but your guy

**⑫ How seriously do you take your guy's promises?**

____ **a.** Not very—he's a big talker who rarely sticks to his word.

____ **b.** Somewhat—he means well when he makes a promise but you can't always count on him to keep it.

____ **c.** Very—he means what he says and you trust him to come through.

# Scoring

Give yourself the numerical value that matches each of your answers. Then add all 12 scores together and use your total score to find your result category.

```
 1. a – 2  b – 3  c – 1
 2. a – 1  b – 2  c – 3
 3. a – 3  b – 1  c – 2
 4. a – 1  b – 2  c – 3
 5. a – 3  b – 2  c – 1
 6. a – 2  b – 3  c – 1
 7. a – 1  b – 2  c – 3
 8. a – 1  b – 2  c – 3
 9. a – 3  b – 1  c – 2
10. a – 2  b – 1  c – 3
11. a – 1  b – 2  c – 3
12. a – 3  b – 2  c – 1
```

**(29–36 points)**

## Go Ahead, Dump Him

Sure, breaking off a relationship is difficult, but let's face it, you and your current chap just aren't suited for each other. In fact he seems pretty hopeless: He shows no interest in really getting to know you (your hopes, dreams, likes, and dislikes); he's not into listening, talking about your feelings, or trying to improve your relationship; and he seems practically allergic to your friends and family. Maybe he's just insecure and uncomfortable around people he doesn't know, but this bad social attitude doesn't bode well for your future together. Basically, he's not offering much, unless all you're looking for is a warm body in bed or a man (*any* man) on your arm. In short, you can do much better. Even going it alone for a while is bound to make you happier than dating Mr. Much-Less-Than-Wonderful.

**(21–28 points)**

## Consider Other Options

Your guy's got a few things going for him, but he's not winning any awards for best boyfriend, either. While he does seem to be trying his best, it may not be good enough for you. Think of him as a fixer-upper, and give some thought to how much time and effort you're willing to put into turning him into a guy you would never even consider dumping. (But keep in mind that there's no guarantee your fixer-upper project will turn out as planned.) If you're not ready to say good-bye to this guy, at least promise yourself you'll keep your options open—and date other men—while you're enjoying what you can about your current relationship.

(12–20 points)
## Don't Let Him Go

What are you—nuts? Why would you even be entertaining the thought of dumping such a great guy? He's basically got all the right moves when it comes to being a dreamboat boyfriend: He's interested in your hopes and dreams; he wants to get to know your friends (and, even cuter, wants them to like him); he's interested in meeting your family; and he's already creating a file in his memory of your likes and dislikes. Plus he seems trustworthy, shows signs of being a decent (if not good) communicator and listener, and he's obviously crazy about you. Unless some other Prince Charming shows up with a glass slipper, you've found your perfect match!

# The Post-Breakup Test: Are You Better Off without Him?

He's gone and all you have left of your relationship are a few photos, lots of memories, and a wide-open social calendar. Before you lament your newly single status, ask yourself this: Are you better off without him? Find out with this test.

**1** **Why did you first fall for your ex?**

____ **a.** He's just such a nice guy, you figured, why not?

____ **b.** He's irresistible—everyone who sees him falls for him.

____ **c.** He had most of the key qualities you've always looked for in a partner.

**2** **When you and your ex were together, Saturday nights were**

____ **a.** Your automatic together time—it was great not to worry about spending weekend nights solo

____ **b.** Repeats of the last Saturday night—you always had fun but could never find more than one or two shared interests

____ **c.** Your automatic together time, even if sometimes you would have rather gone out with your friends

**3** **When you and your ex broke up, your best friend**

____ **a.** Wanted to celebrate having her friend back

____ **b.** Took you out for large scoops of Ben & Jerry's—she didn't want you to cry into your ice cream alone

____ **c.** Told you it was inevitable—he seemed all wrong for you

**4** **When you first introduced your ex to your friends, they**

____ **a.** Teased you about opposites attracting

____ **b.** Wondered what you saw in him (besides his good looks, of course)

____ **c.** Made him feel like one of the gang

**5** **The first time you and your ex celebrated an anniversary (one month, one year, whatever), he**

___ **a.** Took you to a romantic restaurant, but you really wanted to go dancing

___ **b.** Took you to a romantic restaurant—oh, what you wouldn't give for a romantic date like that now

___ **c.** Forgot, then tried to make it up to you in bed

**6** **When you think of your ex now, you**

___ **a.** Wonder who he's sharing his mocha frappuccinos with

___ **b.** Wonder which of your friends you can set him up with

___ **c.** Wonder what you ever saw in him

**7** **Did the M-word (as in marriage) ever come up during your relationship?**

___ **a.** Yes—you both agreed it would be nice, eventually, with someone.

___ **b.** Yes—he firmly expressed his belief in eternal bachelorhood.

___ **c.** No—somehow that word never seemed to relate to the two of you.

**8** **During your relationship, when you had the flu/a cold/a broken bone/whatever, your ex**

___ **a.** Called you every night before he went out with his friends

___ **b.** Kept you company

___ **c.** Paid so much attention to you, you craved some post-recovery space

**9** **If you came across a picture of your ex today, what would you do with it?**

___ **a.** File it in your photo album under "Mr. Not-For-Me"

___ **b.** Toss it

___ **c.** Prop it next to a photo of yourself (for a moment)—you two really did look so good together

**10** **When you and your ex went to parties together**

___ **a.** You loved having him on your arm

___ **b.** You always had fun, but you also couldn't help yourself from checking out available men

___ **c.** You worried so much about him having a good time that you didn't have a good time yourself

# Scoring

Give yourself the numerical value that matches each of your answers. Then add all 10 scores together and use your total score to find your result category.

1. a – 1   b – 3   c – 2
2. a – 2   b – 1   c – 3
3. a – 3   b – 2   c – 1
4. a – 1   b – 3   c – 2
5. a – 1   b – 2   c – 3
6. a – 2   b – 1   c – 3
7. a – 2   b – 3   c – 1
8. a – 3   b – 2   c – 1
9. a – 1   b – 3   c – 2
10. a – 2   b – 1   c – 3

**(24–30 points)**
## You're Happier and Healthier

It's pretty obvious that you're better off without your ex. Now that you're free from his clutches—err, charms—life looks brighter and the future more promising. After all, while physical attraction and sex may not have been lacking, you felt the lack of true connection. How much did you two really have in common? Not much. Besides, when you stop to weigh his positives and negatives, you have to admit that he wouldn't win any personality contests (as your friends will be more than happy to tell you). Chalk this one up to experience and move on.

**(17–23 points)**
## You're Lonely, but You'll Get Over It

Sometimes it's tough to be a single gal in this couples' world. But that's not a good enough reason to make yourself miserable over the end of a relationship that is better over. Plain and simple, if your relationship was meant to be, you'd still be together. Take some time to focus on the reasons you two called it quits instead of daydreaming about the great times you had together (file those thoughts under "nice memories" in your memory bank). Then, as soon as you can, try to get this guy out of your head—you have far better things to think about: your friends, your hobbies, and your career, not to mention the next man in your life!

**(10–16 points)**
## He's a Great Guy, but Not for You

Your ex is a 10, but for you he's a zero. While you may be better off *with* him when it comes to friendship, you're much better off *without* him in the world of love and commitment. Sure, life would be easier if putting two great people together automatically equaled happily ever after, but that's just not the way love works. A strong, healthy romantic relationship requires common interests, shared life goals, passion, friendship, deep love, and much more—much of which you two lacked as a couple. You made the right effort—hey, you've got to give great guys like him a try—but it's time to forget about your ex (or fix him up with a friend!) and move on to someone who's more your style.

# Say Goodbye to Your Ex Test: Are You Ready to Move On?

Take this test to find out if you're ready to meet Mr. Right—or still hung up on Mr. Wrong.

**❶ Your ex's cell phone number is**
____ **a.** Still on your speed dial
____ **b.** Crossed out in your address book
____ **c.** Only available by calling directory assistance

**❷ You're going to a mutual friend's party where you're sure to see your ex. You**
____ **a.** Bring along your most fun and outgoing girlfriend to guarantee a good time (plus she's a great partner for meeting guys!).
____ **b.** Think about what you'll say to him when you first see him. It's important that he sees how cool, calm, and completely over him you are.
____ **c.** Wear your favorite dress—the one that he always complimented you on.

**❸ When your aunt asks about "that charming young man of yours" (she obviously hasn't heard the whole story), you**

____ **a.** Change the subject ASAP
____ **b.** Give her a quick breakup recap then move on to a happier subject, such as how great your job or school is going
____ **c.** Burst into tears

**❹ You find your ex's sweater in your closet. What do you do with it?**
____ **a.** Sleep with it
____ **b.** Clean with it
____ **c.** Donate it

**❺ It's your ex's birthday. You**
____ **a.** Wonder how he's celebrating, then forget about it all in the next minute
____ **b.** Give him a call
____ **c.** Plan a girls' night out *Sex and the City* style!

**❻ When you run into your ex at a mutual friend's wedding, you**
____ **a.** Ask your favorite groomsman to dance

____ **b.** Head straight for the open bar

____ **c.** Introduce him to your incredibly good-looking date

**7** **Your ex just called. You**

____ **a.** Wonder what he wants

____ **b.** Wonder if he's trying to get back together

____ **c.** Wonder why it took him so long to call you back

**8** **When "your song" comes on the radio, you**

____ **a.** Reminisce about the first time you heard it together

____ **b.** Turn it off—you don't need to torture yourself

____ **c.** Don't even realize that it's *that* song until it's almost over

**9** **You walk into a restaurant and spot your ex with another woman. How do you handle it?**

____ **a.** Turn on your heel and split— you've lost your appetite anyway.

____ **b.** Take a deep breath, smile over at him, and sit down at your table.

____ **c.** Go over to say a friendly hello. It would be nice to talk to him (and to check out his date).

**10** **If your ex wanted to get back together, what would you do?**

____ **a.** Agree to meet him for coffee— maybe he *can* change.

____ **b.** Give it another try—there was a reason you got together in the first place.

____ **c.** Think about it for a few minutes, then remind yourself why you broke up.

## Scoring

Give yourself the numerical value that matches each of your answers. Then add all 10 scores together, and use your total score to find your result category.

1. a – 1   b – 2   c – 3
2. a – 3   b – 2   c – 1
3. a – 2   b – 3   c – 1
4. a – 1   b – 2   c – 3
5. a – 3   b – 1   c – 2
6. a – 3   b – 1   c – 2
7. a – 3   b – 2   c – 1
8. a – 1   b – 2   c – 3
9. a – 1   b – 3   c – 2
10. a – 2   b – 1   c – 3

**(24–30 points)**

## Ready for Mr. Right

Congratulations! You survived the breakup, but even better, you've picked yourself up and dusted off that post-relationship rubble. Maybe it took a while, but all that TLC you've given yourself lately has finally paid off. From getting rid of his stuff to finding your place in the Newly Single's Scene, you've captured all the closure you need. Look out, boys, here you come!

**(17–23 points)**

## Looking for Mr. Right Now

Well, there's good news and there's bad news. The good news is that you're halfway there. It probably wasn't pretty, but you've gotten through most of the messy stuff by now. Now for the bad news: Even though you're no longer going through the tissues on a box-a-day basis, you've still got some healing to do. So take it easy, take it slow, and trust yourself to work through it. One word of warning: While a red-hot rebound man might show you a good (and well-deserved) night out, he truly can't cure your ailing heart.

**(10–16 points)**

## Still Stuck on Mr. Wrong

Breaking up is hard to do, and unfortunately no one knows that better than you. If you're still sorting through the "but whys" and "if onlys" (not to mention the secrets and lies), be patient with yourself. Even if you're wondering whether you should get back together, one thing is clear: You need time and TLC from friends and from yourself. Hang in there; your closure will come. In the meantime, try some tried-and-true recovery remedies: luxurious soaks in the bathtub, spending time with people who make you laugh, writing irate letters to your ex and ripping them into shreds, eating well, and celebrating the fact that now you can do things 100 percent *your* way (as opposed to his way) every day.

# 4

# Understand Your Man

**And find out if he's right for you**

Rate Your Date: Should You Go Out with Him Again?

How Hot Is Your Lover in Bed?

Does Your Man Need a Makeover?

Is Your Man Emotionally Stingy?

Is He Ready to Meet the Parents?

# Rate Your Date: Should You Go Out with Him Again?

So how was your date? Should you go out with him again or cut your losses? Answer these questions to find out if another romantic rendezvous is in your future. (Come back and take this quiz again after every date.)

**1** You were ready to roll right on time. Your date

____ **a.** Called to say he'd be a few minutes late

____ **b.** Was right on time

____ **c.** Showed up more than a few minutes late (and didn't call)

**2** Did your date pick you up at your door?

____ **a.** No, we met at a bar.

____ **b.** Yes, he insisted.

____ **c.** Yes, it was on the way.

**3** When he arrived, one of the first things out of his mouth was something like

____ **a.** "You look great."

____ **b.** "Ready to go?"

____ **c.** "I just have to stop at the ATM before we head out" or "Shoot, I forgot my wallet."

**4** Your first thought when he showed up was

____ **a.** He looks okay—nice outfit, not so sure about the hair gel (or vice versa)

____ **b.** I'm dating a fashion misfit

____ **c.** He looks great—nice shirt, nice pants, nice shoes

**5** During your time together, your date

____ **a.** Showed interest in getting to know you

____ **b.** Showed interest in talking about himself

____ **c.** Showed interest in getting to know your waitress

**6** Based on his conversation, you get the sense that your date is

____ **a.** Pretty practical—he talked about where he grew up, career goals, and the high cost of living

___ **b.** Somewhat romantic—he talked about believing in love at first sight, dream trips, and his favorite old movies

___ **c.** Kinda clueless—he talked about how hard it is to meet people, his party days, and going Dutch (as in, wanna go Dutch?)

**7** **Did your date mention his ex?**

___ **a.** Nope, not a word.

___ **b.** Yes, and he seems over her.

___ **c.** Yes, and he doesn't seem over her.

**8** **When did your date's cell phone make its appearance?**

___ **a.** When he called in to check his messages

___ **b.** When it rang and he answered it

___ **c.** Never

**9** **How far did your date try to go sexually?**

___ **a.** Further than I wanted him to

___ **b.** Not far enough

___ **c.** As far as I wanted him to

**10** **Who planned the date?**

___ **a.** He did, and it worked out pretty well.

___ **b.** He did, after asking me what I'd like to do.

___ **c.** I did—he hadn't made any plans when he showed up.

**11** **How did you feel at the end of the date?**

___ **a.** Smitten

___ **b.** Hopeful

___ **c.** Depressed

**12** **When you think about introducing your date to your friends, you**

___ **a.** Can't picture it—he's not their type

___ **b.** Can't decide—who knows what they'll think

___ **c.** Can't wait—they'll love him

**13** **When he talked about work, he**

___ **a.** Raved about his new project

___ **b.** Whined about his boss and his colleagues

___ **c.** Complained about his long hours

**⑭ Conversation during your date was**

____ **a.** Awkward—plenty of lulls, mostly dull moments

____ **b.** Amazing—never a lull, never a dull moment

____ **c.** Friendly—a few lulls, not many dull moments

**⑮ At the end of the evening, he**

____ **a.** Asked if you were free the following weekend

____ **b.** Said he'd call

____ **c.** Said goodnight

# Scoring

Give yourself the numerical value that matches each of your answers. Then add all 15 scores together and use your total score to find your result category.

1. a – 2   b – 3   c – 1
2. a – 1   b – 3   c – 2
3. a – 3   b – 2   c – 1
4. a – 2   b – 1   c – 3
5. a – 1   b – 2   c – 3
6. a – 2   b – 3   c – 1
7. a – 3   b – 2   c – 1
8. a – 1   b – 2   c – 3
9. a – 1   b – 2   c – 3
10. a – 2   b – 3   c – 1
11. a – 3   b – 2   c – 1
12. a – 1   b – 2   c – 3
13. a – 3   b – 1   c – 2
14. a – 1   b – 3   c – 2
15. a – 3   b – 2   c – 1

(35–45 points)

## He's a Winner!

You already know that your date went well. You two seem to have really hit it off. He's nice, respectful, interesting, and—maybe most important at this stage—interested in you. And it sounds like you won't have to worry about making over his wardrobe (what a relief) or teaching him the finer points of dating etiquette. So, go out again (and again) and have fun. Your Saturday nights are looking sweet!

(25–34 points)

## He's Worth Another Date

While your date may not have made the *best* impression, he didn't make the worst either. He seems like a nice enough guy. You two did enjoy decent date conversation, right? If he calls and asks you out again, what do you have to lose? Go ahead, give him another chance.

(15–24 points)

## He's a Loser

To be blunt, you'd probably have a better time staying at home washing your hair than going out with this guy again. You'd probably have a better time scrubbing your bathroom tiles with a toothbrush than struggling through another outing with a guy who doesn't know the first thing about how to behave on a date. Why waste your time with him when there are so many other (better) dates out there?

# How Hot Is Your Lover in Bed?

Sexual compatibility in a relationship is important for long-term happiness and, of course, sexual satisfaction. While sex does not equal love, it is a major factor in the equation. How does your partner rate in the sexual skills department? Take this quiz and find out if he's a passion master or in need of intimacy instruction.

**1** Do you feel comfortable communicating your sexual desires to your partner?

____ **a.** Not really—he doesn't like to talk about such intimate details.

____ **b.** Yes, he always listens and tries to please you.

____ **c.** No, he gets defensive (as if you're criticizing him) when you mention what you'd like in bed.

**2** When it comes to pleasuring you, your partner

____ **a.** Pays more attention to his own pleasure

____ **b.** Focuses on you *after* he has climaxed

____ **c.** Goes out of his way to satisfy you sexually

**3** What could your partner do to make your sex life more enjoyable?

____ **a.** Learn some new lovemaking tricks to add extra excitement

____ **b.** Be more sensitive to your needs and desires

____ **c.** Stop pressuring you to have sex

**4** You and your partner connect in bed about as well as

____ **a.** Oil and water—you seem to be on different planets half the time

____ **b.** Fuel and fire—your sex life is hot and passionate

____ **c.** Gin and tonic—your connection is natural, your sex life predictable

**5** How often do you have an orgasm?

____ **a.** Regularly

____ **b.** Never

____ **c.** Sometimes

**⑥ Which of the following statements is most true for you?**

____ **a.** Your sex life is practically nonexistent.

____ **b.** Your sex life has become routine and even a little bit boring.

____ **c.** Your sex life is just as good as it was in the beginning of your relationship.

**⑦ The thought of making love to your partner makes you feel**

____ **a.** Excited—you and your partner have great chemistry and know how to please each other

____ **b.** Closer to him—during sex is when he's the most affectionate and loving

____ **c.** Anxious—it takes so much work for you to reach orgasm (if you do at all)

**⑧ When it comes to kissing, caressing, and other forms of foreplay during lovemaking, your partner**

____ **a.** Does a little kissing and touching to get started, then expects you to be ready for intercourse

____ **b.** Knows how, where, and when to kiss and caress you to please you sexually

____ **c.** Seems to have forgotten how important those elements are to lovemaking

**⑨ What do you wish your partner knew about you sexually that he doesn't already know?**

____ **a.** Everything—he's pretty clueless about how your body and mind work when it comes to lovemaking.

____ **b.** That you don't get turned on as quickly and automatically as he does!

____ **c.** Nothing—he's really good at learning and satisfying your needs and desires.

## Scoring

Give yourself the numerical value that matches each of your answers. Then add all nine scores together and use your total score to find your result category.

1. a – 2   b – 3   c – 1
2. a – 1   b – 2   c – 3
3. a – 3   b – 2   c – 1
4. a – 1   b – 3   c – 2
5. a – 3   b – 1   c – 2
6. a – 1   b – 2   c – 3
7. a – 3   b – 2   c – 1

8. **a** – 2  **b** – 3  **c** – 1
9. **a** – 1  **b** – 2  **c** – 3

**(22–27 points)**

## He's Hot

You and your partner have a passionate sex life, thanks to obvious chemistry and a mutual desire to please each other. You're comfortable talking about sex with your love mate (a huge plus) because he's open to hearing your commendations as well as any constructive criticism (if you express it nicely). With someone next to you in bed who goes out of his way to satisfy you sexually, you're one lucky woman!

**(15–21 points)**

## He's Warm

Your lover may not be boiling between the sheets but he's not ice-cold, either. While the two of you share a comfortable (yawn) sex life, there's definitely room for improvement, especially when it comes to *your* pleasure. It's high time your man understood your body and knew your sexual wants and needs. How can you get him to sat-isfy you sexually? You're going to have to get vocal or at least figure out a way to *show* him what works best for you in bed. That's the only way you're going to turn him into a better lover—and you into a contented woman.

**(9–14 points)**

## He's Cold

A little breezy in your bedroom, huh? While he may love you, he doesn't know how to show that love between the sheets. A healthy, happy sex life requires open, honest communication about your sexual desires and a mutual desire to please each other. It's time to turn your love life around. How do you go about getting what you want from your lover? Most men aren't all that open to criticism or even instruction when it comes to sex, so you're going to have to be careful. First figure out what *you* want for a happy sex life. Then tell him something you *like* about your love-making—or about his body, his smile, whatever. Starting out on a positive note will help it go more smoothly. Good luck!

# Does Your Man Need a Makeover?

It's natural for you to want your guy to look his best. But because it's tough to get most guys to change their ways, it's good to know how much he needs a makeover before you struggle to transform him. Find out his makeover requirements—plus how to polish his look without too much fuss.

**1** **The last time your honey got a haircut was**

____ **a.** You have no idea—you never know what's going on underneath his baseball cap

____ **b.** Several months ago

____ **c.** Last month

____ **d.** Last week

**2** **His nicest shoes are**

____ **a.** A sturdy pair, nice enough for work or a night out

____ **b.** An outdated pair of loafers or wingtips

____ **c.** Handsome and stylish, and a little expensive

____ **d.** A scuffed pair of boots or sneakers

**3** **You'd say that his biggest grooming flaw is**

____ **a.** He hates giving more than two seconds' thought to grooming, period

____ **b.** He spends too much time on his appearance

____ **c.** He neglects the details, such as nice socks or a nice scent

____ **d.** His style dates from the eighties—and not in a cool, retro way

**4** **His *best* outfit (the one he wears when he has to look nice) is**

____ **a.** A shirt or sweater that looks good on him, with his best shoes and pants

____ **b.** A sweater his mom bought him in college and a pair of not-too-worn pants

____ **c.** Pants that don't quite fit anymore and a tie you'd secretly like to bury in the backyard

____ **d.** A swanky suit

**5** His *favorite* outfit (the one he'd wear every day if he could) is

____ **a.** A stylish and casual pair of pants with a great shirt

____ **b.** A comfy sweater and khakis or jeans

____ **c.** Jeans and a T-shirt with a well-worn flannel or leather jacket

____ **d.** Sweatpants or faded jeans and a sweatshirt that looks like it's been through a war

**6** If you could compare your guy's style to a movie character's, whose would it be?

____ **a.** Mike Myers in *Wayne's World*

____ **b.** Woody Allen in . . . well, anything

____ **c.** Hugh Grant in *Four Weddings and a Funeral*

____ **d.** Jude Law in *The Talented Mr. Ripley*

**7** If you could change one thing about the way your sweetie puts himself together, it would be

____ **a.** His hair or his shoes—otherwise, he looks okay

____ **b.** His clothes—his wardrobe needs a serious update

____ **c.** His attitude—the guy just refuses to think about style

____ **d.** His obsessive perfectionism about his appearance

**8** How responsive is your guy to gentle suggestions about his appearance?

____ **a.** He'd be surprised if you had anything negative to say.

____ **b.** He couldn't care less about his looks, so suggestions roll right off him.

____ **c.** He's sensitive but willing to listen.

____ **d.** He's pretty sensitive, almost defensive.

**9** What's his overall attitude about his personal style?

____ **a.** "Whatever."

____ **b.** "I'm not so sure about fashion stuff."

____ **c.** "I'm pretty sure I look good."

____ **d.** "I'm confident I look good."

# Scoring

Give yourself the numerical value that matches each of your answers. Then add all nine scores together and use your total score to find your result category.

1. a – 4   b – 3   c – 2   d – 1
2. a – 2   b – 3   c – 1   d – 4
3. a – 4   b – 1   c – 2   d – 3
4. a – 2   b – 4   c – 3   d – 1
5. a – 1   b – 2   c – 3   d – 4
6. a – 4   b – 3   c – 2   d – 1
7. a – 2   b – 3   c – 4   d – 1
8. a – 1   b – 4   c – 2   d – 3
9. a – 4   b – 3   c – 2   d – 1

(31–36 points)

## Fashion *Fuhgeddaboutit*

Your guy may have a slob superiority complex! He doesn't want to waste time or energy on what he considers trivial—appearance. While you can encourage a man to change his shirt, it's much harder to encourage him to change himself. In the end, it's his decision whether or not to clean up his act, but you may want to remind him that attention to grooming is one of many ways evolved primates demonstrate respect for each other. If his slovenly looks make you feel seriously uncomfortable in a social setting and he's unresponsive to tactful, uncritical suggestions, exercise a little tough love. If he can't be bothered to put on a clean shirt, you don't have to make excuses for him, include him in your invitations, or even stand next to him at Grandma's buffet table.

(24–30 points)

## Fashion Freakout

Chances are your guy is skittish about the whole "dressing up" thing. He wishes he knew more about how to put himself together, but since he doesn't, he flip-flops between pretending he doesn't care and pretending he knows what he's doing. Either way, it's a touchy subject. Your challenge is to repair his fashion sense without hurting his feelings. Step one is calming his anxiety: Be casual (not critical). Step two is becoming his confidante: Let him know what you think looks good on him, and ask him to do the same for you. Step three—without skipping one or two—is to take the burden on *both* of your shoulders. Go on a shopping trip together and ask his advice before offering yours. Surprise him with a sweater you think will look great on him. Once he knows you're a dependable, friendly source of information, and not a fashion dictator, your makeover suggestions will build his self-confidence instead of undermining it.

(16–23 points)
## Fashion Fixer-Upper

Your sweetie is stylish—almost. He's got an idea of what looks good on him, and he's on the right track. What he may skip sometimes are the things that seem like too much trouble, such as getting his hair cut, wearing nice socks, or picking the right tie. You can offer a subtle helping hand by pulling the details together. Take a friendly, flirty (not critical) approach to helping him get ready for parties or family gatherings. Rather than telling him what to wear, tell him which of his ties you like, or how great he looks when he styles his hair just so. Make it

clear that what you love about a "sharp-dressed man" is that the sharp-dressed man is *him*. He may be grateful that you took the time to help him shine.

(9–15 points)
## Fashion Fanatic

Your man is either really well put-together—or he really, really thinks he is. Either way, you'll face a challenge if you want to convince him to change anything about his looks. If he's a man of sartorial savvy, congratulations—we'll see him in *GQ*'s "Best Dressed" issue! But if your man feels rock solid about his appearance even though he's standing on the San Andreas Fault of style, it may be better to grin and bear it than wound his pride. When you stride into the room on his arm, remember that real style is all about self-confidence.

# Is Your Man Emotionally Stingy?

No one likes a cheapskate—not when it comes to matters of the wallet, and certainly not the heart. Use this quiz to find out if your guy is generous or stingy with his affections.

**1** **If you were to grab your guy's hand in public, he would probably**

____ **a.** Squeeze your hand right back

____ **b.** Hold your hand for a quick second, then let go

____ **c.** Tell you he doesn't like public displays of affection

**2** **The last time your guy gave you a gift, it was**

____ **a.** Expensive but pretty impersonal

____ **b.** Exactly what you wanted—you couldn't believe that he remembered

____ **c.** Romantic and sweet

**3** **When you're choosing a restaurant for dinner, he usually**

____ **a.** Makes a reservation at one of your favorite places

____ **b.** Makes a reservation at one of his favorite places, even if you don't care for it

____ **c.** Suggests a few of his favorite spots, then asks where you'd like to go

**4** **He loves sending his friends and family e-cards because**

____ **a.** They're creative—he loves the animation and the music.

____ **b.** They're convenient—who has time to sift through card racks in a store?

____ **c.** E-cards? He doesn't send any kind of card, ever.

**5** **You've had a really hard day. When you see your guy and tell him about it, he**

____ **a.** Tells you about his day

____ **b.** Says he's sorry to hear it

____ **c.** Gives you a hug or offers to massage your back to help you relax

**6** Does your guy usually remember special dates?

____ **a.** Yes—he loves to celebrate everything from Valentine's Day to your anniversary.

____ **b.** No—he just seems to forget all about them.

____ **c.** Sometimes—he knows they're important to you, so he definitely makes an effort.

**7** When your guy greets his male friends (especially after not seeing them for a while), he usually

____ **a.** Shakes hands

____ **b.** Combines a pat on the back with a shake of the hand

____ **c.** Does the manly hug thing—fast, strong embrace

**8** Does your man contact you during the day?

____ **a.** Yes—he tells you he's thinking about you or just says hello.

____ **b.** Sometimes—if he has something he wants to share with you or ask you.

____ **c.** No—he's too busy to even think of you during the day.

**9** The last time you both got dressed up for a night on the town, what did he say when he first saw you?

____ **a.** "That's a nice dress."

____ **b.** "Are you ready?"

____ **c.** "Wow, you look great!"

**10** When your guy goes grocery shopping, he

____ **a.** Stocks up on the basics.

____ **b.** Almost always picks up something he knows you like.

____ **c.** Grocery shopping? Ha! He counts on you to keep him fed.

## Scoring

Give yourself the numerical value that matches each of your answers. Then add all 10 scores together and use your total score to find your result category.

1. a – 3   b – 2   c – 1
2. a – 1   b – 3   c – 2
3. a – 3   b – 1   c – 2
4. a – 3   b – 2   c – 1
5. a – 1   b – 2   c – 3
6. a – 3   b – 1   c – 2
7. a – 1   b – 2   c – 3

8. a – 3   b – 2   c – 1
9. a – 2   b – 1   c – 3
10. a – 2   b – 3   c – 1

(24–30 points)
## Generous Joe

Lucky you. You've snagged a man with an expressive heart and a generous spirit. No doubt your guy pays his own way in life and prides himself on being strong and self-sufficient. But that doesn't stop him from showing his sensitive side at appropriate moments. His generosity when it comes to giving in terms of affection and admiration translates to material items, too (dinner, movie tickets, gifts). Enjoy it and be sure to show your gratitude—and do your fair share of giving, too.

(18–23 points)
## Cost-Conscious Carl

You can't blame a guy for being careful with his money. But you can fault him for holding back emotionally. Your guy isn't completely without feeling, but he has a hard time expressing himself, which can be frustrating when you're looking for signs that he's into you. Not to mention the fact that it's difficult to be giving yourself when you're getting so little in return. If you can encourage him to be a bit more open, you'll both enjoy the relationship more. Remind him that a healthy relationship is based on give-and-take on a variety of fronts (which doesn't mean that one person *gives* while the other *takes*). In the meantime, be careful that you're not stopping yourself (or letting him stop you) from enjoying the pleasures in life.

(10–17 points)
## Cheapskate Charlie

Wake up, grab your wallet, and run! Your man is cheap emotionally. While there's nothing wrong with a man who is smart and careful with his money, a man who is miserly with his affection is no fun—and usually incapable of a truly close relationship. Where does that leave you? Giving a lot and getting very little in return. Do yourself a favor: Find a new man to shower with affection—someone who will be equally generous in return.

# Is He Ready to Meet the Parents?

Should you invite your new man home? Whether you're newly in love or just in deep "like," this quiz will help you decide if it's time for Mr. Potentially Right to meet Mom and Dad.

**1** How long have you and your man been seeing each other?

____ **a.** Not long—he's seen only your two cutest outfits

____ **b.** For several great months

____ **c.** Longer than your last boyfriend, but shorter than a season of *Sex and the City*

**2** Which "L" word has your boyfriend whispered in your ear so far?

____ **a.** Love, as in, "I ____ you."

____ **b.** Love, as in "I ____ that lacy thing you wore to bed last night."

____ **c.** Lunch, as in "Let's have ____."

**3** The common refrain of friends who have met your current flame is

____ **a.** "Are you kidding me?"

____ **b.** "He's a huge improvement over the last one."

____ **c.** "He's a keeper."

**4** In your mind, what's the worst thing that could happen when your boyfriend and parents meet?

____ **a.** Your mom will tell an embarrassing story about you as a naked baby.

____ **b.** Your boyfriend will tell an embarrassing story about you as a naked lady.

____ **c.** He'll wear that tacky sweater you hate.

**5** You and your boyfriend most resemble this TV twosome:

____ **a.** Monica and Chandler on *Friends:* romantic and fun loving

____ **b.** Joey and Phoebe on *Friends:* definitely close, but it's hard to see where they're going

____ **c.** Ross and Rachel on *Friends:* deeply connected but with lots of drama

**6** If you were to stay over at your parents' house, how would he handle the sleeping arrangements?

____ **a.** He'd explain to your parents that you are red-hot lovers and make a beeline for your bedroom.

____ **b.** He'd follow along with what your parents want.

____ **c.** He'd take your father aside and ask his permission to sleep in your room.

**7** Meeting a girlfriend's parents is stressful at best. How well does your guy cope with pressure?

____ **a.** Not well—he might as well have "Johnny Road Rage" on his driver's license.

____ **b.** You've only seen him mildly stressed so far, but you have high hopes for his coping ability—stuck in a traffic jam, he'd probably mutter a bit but wouldn't curse like a lunatic.

____ **c.** You've seen him at his most stressed out and there were no tears, screaming, or fist fights.

**8** At this early stage, your relationship compatibility level is

____ **a.** Pretty good—you agree on big things (such as, marriage and family are important goals) but have a variety of little issues to iron out

____ **b.** Amazing—you're possible soul mates

____ **c.** Shaky—if it weren't for the physical chemistry, things probably wouldn't have gotten this far

**9** Your parents are so desperate for you to get married, they've already put aside a deposit for a reception hall. How will your boyfriend react to their not-so-subtle suggestions that he cough up a ring?

____ **a.** He'll probably make a few jokes that will put everyone at ease.

____ **b.** It's 50/50 that he'll make a run for it and never be heard from again.

____ **c.** It might shake him a bit, but you're pretty sure he'll realize it's them talking, not you.

**10** Has your boyfriend invited you to meet his parents?

____ **a.** Um, he hasn't even mentioned that he has parents (or siblings, or friends).

____ **b.** Yes, and you got along beautifully.

____ **c.** No, but you have met a few of his friends.

**11** What do *you* think his meeting your parents means?

____ **a.** Things are getting serious, and your family should meet the man you just might spend the rest of your life with.

____ **b.** It will be a nice meal where he will learn more about you.

____ **c.** You're finally satisfying Mom and Dad's request to bring a guy home to meet them.

**12** What do you think *he* thinks his meeting your parents means?

____ **a.** Things are getting serious, and your family should meet the man you just might spend the rest of your life with.

____ **b.** He'll enjoy a nice meal where he will learn more about you.

____ **c.** He'll get a free meal.

## Scoring

Give yourself the numerical value that matches each of your answers. Then add all 12 scores together and use your total score to find your result category.

```
 1. a – 1  b – 3  c – 2
 2. a – 3  b – 2  c – 1
 3. a – 1  b – 2  c – 3
 4. a – 2  b – 1  c – 3
 5. a – 3  b – 1  c – 2
 6. a – 1  b – 3  c – 2
 7. a – 1  b – 2  c – 3
 8. a – 2  b – 3  c – 1
 9. a – 3  b – 1  c – 2
10. a – 1  b – 3  c – 2
11. a – 3  b – 2  c – 1
12. a – 3  b – 2  c – 1
```

(28–36 points)

## Packaged for Parents

This guy is made for parental viewing. He's polite, successful, intelligent, funny, and can take in stride Mom and Dad's sometimes overbearing attempts at getting their princess a permanent partner. More signs of promise: He treats you like a queen, is unafraid of the "L" word, and has introduced you to his folks. No doubt he also shares your values and goals. He can definitely take meeting your folks. And a man who hangs around after seeing your chubby baby pics and eating your mom's stale crumb cake is a man worth hanging onto.

(20–27 points)

## Not Quite Ready for Parental Viewing

Things appear promising, but it's best you give it a little more time before subjecting this relatively new boyfriend to the parental microscope. Even though you've discovered common goals, he's still untested (you haven't seen him in a serious pressure situation).

When two people are still determining if what they share is more than lust, they should remain in their new-couple cocoon. It's fine to get together with friends, but why raise your parents' hopes when you're not sure he's "the one"? If your parents are pressuring you, tell them when things are on a potentially serious track, you'll bring him around. Warning them that they may scare the guy away should quiet them down.

(12–19 points)

## For Non-Parental Eyes Only

The guy must be easy on the eyes or great in bed because physical seems to be your main connection. Since he hasn't opened his life to you in any meaningful way (by, for example, introducing you to people he cares about), he's not ready to meet the folks. If you want to continue seeing him, that's fine as long as you recognize and can easily handle the limitations (that he may be a commitment-phobe with a low tolerance for stressful situations). If you seek a man who can make a good partner, you can cut your losses now, or ride out the relationship and see where it takes you. Giving him the benefit of the doubt, it could be too early to determine whether Mr. Right Now is a potential Mr. Right.

# 5

# Check Your Couple Compatibility

**And find out if your love will last**

Are You and Your Mate Meant to Be?

What Kind of Couple Are You?

What's Your Fighting Style?

Are You a Relationship Wimp?

Can Your Relationship Survive the Long-Distance Test?

# Are You and Your Mate Meant to Be?

No relationship is perfect, but there are signs that indicate that two people are especially compatible. Are you and your man meant to be together? Take this test and find out if your relationship will last.

**1** **When you and your mate want to spend a romantic evening together, you**

____ **a.** Almost always agree on what would make for the perfect night

____ **b.** Usually disagree about what's romantic and what you should do

____ **c.** Make sure to do a little something you enjoy and a little something he enjoys

**2** **If your man were to send you flowers, they would probably be**

____ **a.** Whatever's in season

____ **b.** A dozen roses—it's hard to go wrong with this classic

____ **c.** Exactly the kind that you love

**3** **What's the first thing you would do after returning from a weeklong trip away from your honey?**

____ **a.** Give him a kiss

____ **b.** Ask about his week while leafing through the mail

____ **c.** Call your mother

**4** **What's the first thing your guy would do after returning from a weeklong trip away from you?**

____ **a.** Give you a kiss

____ **b.** Ask about your week while leafing through the mail

____ **c.** Call his mother

**5** **When you and your S.O. argue, you**

____ **a.** Keep your distance from each other until the anger subsides

____ **b.** Complain to your friends but never seem to resolve the issue together

____ **c.** Usually talk it out and make up fairly quickly

**6** When you want to know how your guy really feels about you, you

____ **a.** Hint around, trying to get him to say something positive

____ **b.** Wait it out—you'd only annoy him if you bothered him with silly questions

____ **c.** Ask him

**7** You and your man are out to dinner with another couple. You're discussing a controversial subject and the three of them all agree, but you don't. When you assert your opinion, your S.O.

____ **a.** Puts you down or waves off what you say

____ **b.** Stares at his food

____ **c.** Encourages you to make your point

**8** What do you and your man argue about?

____ **a.** Important things—how you save and spend money, whether you're both ready to commit/marry/have kids

____ **b.** Various things—one partner working too much, which one of you is a better driver

____ **c.** Every little thing—where to eat dinner, the way he might look at the waitress when you get there

**9** During a girls' night out, the man of your dreams (handsome, funny, charming, and attracted to you!) hits on you. If there were no way your partner could ever find out, would you cheat on him?

____ **a.** Probably—what would it hurt?

____ **b.** Never!

____ **c.** You doubt it—it wouldn't be worth it

**10** You sometimes look at your single friends with

____ **a.** Empathy—you know how tough it is to be single

____ **b.** Pity—you can't help it, you know how great it feels to be in love

____ **c.** Envy—you can't help it, their lives seem like so much fun

**11** If you spotted your man talking to an attractive woman at a party, you would

____ **a.** Find other people to socialize with

____ **b.** Join him and make sure the woman knows you're a couple

____ **c.** Ask him if he's more interested in her than in you

**12** If you went out with the girls and forgot to call your partner to tell him you'd be late, how would he react?

____ **a.** He'd be suspicious of what you were up to.

____ **b.** He might not even notice.

____ **c.** He'd be worried about you.

**13** The word that best fits the way you feel about your guy is

____ **a.** Love—and it feels great

____ **b.** Need—you can't imagine getting through a day without him

____ **c.** Like—definitely *strong* like

**14** Your friends and family think your partner is

____ **a.** A good guy, but they still need to get to know him better

____ **b.** Pretty terrific—they've formed quite an impression by now

____ **c.** Nonexistent—they haven't even met him

# Scoring

Give yourself the numerical value that matches each of your answers. Then add all 14 scores together and use the total score to find your result category.

1. a – 3  b – 1  c – 2
2. a – 1  b – 2  c – 3
3. a – 3  b – 2  c – 1
4. a – 3  b – 2  c – 1
5. a – 2  b – 1  c – 3
6. a – 2  b – 1  c – 3
7. a – 1  b – 2  c – 3
8. a – 3  b – 2  c – 1
9. a – 1  b – 3  c – 2
10. a – 2  b – 3  c – 1
11. a – 3  b – 2  c – 1
12. a – 1  b – 2  c – 3
13. a – 3  b – 1  c – 2
14. a – 2  b – 3  c – 1

(33–42 points)
## Just-about-Perfect Pair

You two make a great match. Your relationship is healthy and strong, mostly because you work hard at making it so. You're honest with each other, communicate clearly, and seem to respect and appreciate each other—all crucial characteristics of a good relationship. In addition you're self-confident and you trust your man, which lets you live your own life (and lets him do the same) and avoid the petty jealousies and possession problems that plague other couples. Keep it up and you two will be together for a long time.

(24–32 points)

## Promising Pair

Your relationship has its strong points but its problems as well. While no relationship is perfect, you and your man would be wise to work on the tricky things that seem to be holding you back from made-for-each-other happiness. Take a look at how you interact. For example, do you say what's on your mind or expect him to guess what you're thinking? Close couples know how to communicate well—they don't play mind games or have unrealistic ideals. Keep in mind, too, that a healthy relationship requires that both partners respect, trust, and appreciate each other. If you and your partner can work on those key areas, you'll go from promising to just-about-perfect in no time.

(14–23 points)

## Poor Pair

Honestly, it's a wonder you two are together. Your relationship appears to be missing most of the critical characteristics of strong, healthy couples. You may already know this—and no doubt you're pretty unhappy. You may be trying to fool yourself into thinking you and your partner are better suited for each other than you really are, perhaps because you dread being single again. But it's time to face facts, and all the signs seem to point to you and your partner being a poor pair. Your relationship lacks trust, respect, and fondness for each other. While you could work to fix your considerable problems, you're probably better off cutting your losses and finding someone you feel more comfortable with.

# What Kind of Couple Are You?

There are many kinds of couples, but marriage and family counselors tend to think about *all* couples as one of two different types—complementary or symmetrical. Take this test to find out which style best describes you and your partner, and what that says about your relationship.

**1** When it comes to socializing as a couple

____ **a.** One of you generally makes all the social plans

____ **b.** Both of you arrange different activities at different times

**2** How do the two of you handle chores at home?

____ **a.** You divide the labor—you each have a set task list.

____ **b.** You deal with things on an "as needed" basis—whoever's free deals with the task at hand.

**3** Does the same person almost always take the wheel when you're together in the car?

____ **a.** Yes

____ **b.** No

**4** In your relationship, do each of you have clearly defined roles?

____ **a.** Yes

____ **b.** No

**5** Who pays the bills in your relationship?

____ **a.** Typically the same person each month

____ **b.** The one who has the money at the time

**6** In your relationship, do you follow fairly traditional male and female role models?

____ **a.** Yes

____ **b.** No

**7** When it comes to free time on weekends you

___ **a.** Generally do most things together
___ **b.** Often do separate activities

**8** Would you say that you two share relationship responsibilities equally?

___ **a.** No
___ **b.** Yes

**9** When it comes to cooking

___ **a.** Generally only one of you does it
___ **b.** You share and enjoy cooking activities

**10** You would describe the two of you as

___ **a.** A leader and a follower
___ **b.** Colleagues sharing a project

## Scoring

Give yourself the numerical value that matches each of your answers. Then add all 10 scores together and use your total score to find your result category.

1. **a – 2  b – 1**
2. **a – 2  b – 1**
3. **a – 2  b – 1**
4. **a – 2  b – 1**
5. **a – 2  b – 1**
6. **a – 2  b – 1**
7. **a – 2  b – 1**
8. **a – 2  b – 1**
9. **a – 2  b – 1**
10. **a – 2  b – 1**

(15–20 points)
## Complementary Style

In a complementary relationship "two parts make the whole." Each partner has separate areas that are exclusively his or her domain. To this couple, it is obvious who works and who manages the home, who cooks and who pays the bills. This style of relationship is comfortable and predictable—each person knows his or her role and job within the relationship—but it can be *too* predictable. The roles may be so clearly separated that the partners grow to feel trapped in their respective roles and unable to ask the other for input or assistance. Experiment with some symmetrical style behaviors. Let the social planner take a weekend off while the other partner does some scheduling. Or swap duties for a day. You may find that your skills extend beyond what you previously thought, and you may find new enjoyable activities to do together—or apart.

(10–14 points)
## Symmetrical Style

In a symmetrical relationship, both partners view themselves as equal partners. Either partner may take on virtually any role, depending on the situation. The symmetrical style has the advantage of keeping life interesting—you never know in advance who is going to do what, and each situation is a new opportunity. The disadvantage is that every new challenge can involve a decision or debate about who is going to take the initiative.

Experiment with some complementary style behaviors. Divide some regular duties and see if it makes tasks easier to accomplish. Or choose an activity to do together on a weekend and see if you enjoy the together time.

*NOTE:* While neither relationship style—complementary or symmetrical—is better than the other, marriage and family counselors often look for the signs that a relationship is fluid over time: that the relationship transitions from complementary to symmetrical and back again. The strength of a relationship is in the ability to learn new styles and new possibilities of relating, rather than getting stuck in one form or another.

# What's Your Fighting Style?

Conflict and the angry feelings that go with it are inevitable in marriage. It's how a couple handles angry feelings that determines whether or not their relationship will endure. Answer these questions to find out your arguing attitude and what you can do to achieve relationship harmony.

**1** **Your partner accuses you of doing something that upset him, but you don't think you did anything wrong. What do you do?**

____ **a.** Use that opportunity to bring up something he did that upset you.

____ **b.** Apologize anyway—he's probably right that you were in the wrong.

____ **c.** Ask him to explain why he thinks you were wrong, so you can understand what you did—and try not to do it again.

____ **d.** Say something like, "Of course I was wrong, I'm always wrong, aren't I!" and stomp out of the room—you hate how he's always blaming you for everything.

**2** **During an argument with your partner, you often**

____ **a.** Rehash old points of conflict

____ **b.** Fail to make the point you were trying to make

____ **c.** Ask your partner to explain his feelings, and do the same yourself

____ **d.** Say things you regret later

**3** **You wish your partner would show you more affection. What do you do?**

____ **a.** Accuse him of not loving you anymore—if he did, he would be more affectionate.

____ **b.** Nothing—you can't change him.

____ **c.** Tell him you'd like it if he showed you more affection, and give a few examples.

____ **d.** Say to him, "You're as romantic as a stuffed doll!"

**4** Your husband forgets to tell you that he has to work all weekend. If you'd known in advance that you'd be the only parent on duty, you would have arranged the kids' schedule to make it easier. You can't help feeling steamed. What do you do?

____ **a.** Say, "You owe me big time, buddy—next weekend, I'm out of here and you're in charge!"

____ **b.** Remind yourself that it's not his fault he has to work.

____ **c.** Make sure he understands before he leaves why you're so upset—with any luck, next time he'll remember to warn you about such plans ahead of time.

____ **d.** Say, "You're so selfish—don't you ever think about anyone else but yourself?"

**5** At a party, you catch your mate paying special attention to an attractive blonde, so you

____ **a.** Find a handsome man to flirt with and make sure your mate notices

____ **b.** Socialize in another room—there's no reason you have to watch him acting like an idiot

____ **c.** Wait until you're driving home and tell him how terrible it makes you feel when he pays more attention to other women than he does to you

____ **d.** Walk right up to him and say, "Maybe you'd rather go home with her than me!"

**6** Your children have left their toys/books/clothes all over the place and your husband let them go outside to play without cleaning up. When you confront the mess, you

____ **a.** Appoint your husband Mr. Clean Up—maybe next time he'll get the kids to do it

____ **b.** Clean it up yourself—no one else is going to do it

____ **c.** Ask your husband how he thinks it makes you feel when he fails to discipline the kids

____ **d.** Ask, "Are your eyes not working today—do you not see this mess?"

**7** Your partner has failed to do the dinner dishes again, and you wake up to a mess. What do you do?

____ **a.** Threaten never to cook again if he leaves one more dirty dish in the sink!

____ **b.** Toss everything into the dishwasher just to get it out of your sight.

____ **c.** Tell him that next time you'd really appreciate it if he would take care of the dishes before bed because it ruins your day to wake up to a mess.

____ **d.** Storm out of the house without speaking to him.

**8** **How often do you raise your voice during a fight with your partner?**

____ **a.** As often as you need to—sometimes that's the only way to get your point across.

____ **b.** Almost never—you know your partner doesn't like it.

____ **c.** Rarely—you'd rather talk it out than yell at each other.

____ **d.** Often—your blood boils and you can't help screaming.

**9** **Which fighting strategy are you most apt to use?**

____ **a.** Withholding sex to get your way, or tears—these tactics always get him.

____ **b.** Apologizing just to smooth things over—you hate arguing.

____ **c.** Talk, talk, and more talk.

____ **d.** Yelling, yelling, and more yelling— how else can you really get his attention?

# Scoring

Add up the number of As, Bs, Cs, and Ds you chose. Find the category in which you had the most responses to determine your fighting style. Also check out your secondary arguing attitude, based on your next highest number of responses.

(Mostly As)
## Manipulator

Apologizing and compromising are not in your repertoire. You'll do just about anything—from turning the blame around to bringing up long-dead issues—to win an argument. Manipulation may seem like the only path to getting your way, but in the end, it backfires. The manipulated spouse feels angry, and that anger can cause him to get defensive or to withdraw, neither of which helps solve the problem. You may use this fighting style because you feel that your partner has all the power. Manipulation, the only power play you know, is your way of trying to even the score. The next time, try a new tack: discussion. Say goodbye to defending, justifying, and counterattacking (turning the tables). To have a healthy discussion, take turns being the speaker and the listener. The next time, let the partner with the gripe go first.

Don't worry, the listener will get a turn to be heard. When the speaker feels completely heard and understood, it's time to switch roles. Keep in mind that good listeners convey, in various ways, that they have heard and understood what has been said and do not pass judgment. Remember that listening is the cement of a happy marriage!

(Mostly Bs)
### Avoider

You're a yielder—you attempt to resolve conflicts by surrendering on issues, even those important to you. Why? You may fear confrontation or abandonment or be afraid to make your partner angry. Or you may simply want to be liked, because of low self-esteem. You try to convince yourself that if the problem is ignored it will go away. But problems don't disappear. They get worse, because your silent acceptance of your partner's behavior leads him to continue, which will continue to hurt and anger you. And your resentment will invariably ooze to the surface and cause more conflict. You need to address problems directly. Speak up when you have a problem and state your needs, something many women aren't very

good at. The next time you are upset with your mate, fight off your desire to let it pass and force yourself to speak up. If that's too difficult, write a letter to your partner, expressing what's bothering you. Stay cool (wait until you're calm to broach the topic); discuss one issue at a time (not everything that's wrong in your relationship); think before you speak (say only what you know will be constructive and lead you toward a resolution); and remember your goal—resolution, not demolishing your mate.

(Mostly Cs)
### Talker

You're a born orator. And most of the time, your talking skills manage to calm conflicts before they turn into all-out fights. You're not one to walk away from an argument without fully explaining your feelings—and getting your partner to spill too. Being so open is great, but if you're finding that your partner doesn't always comprehend, you may be talking too soon and possibly too much. If your partner is hurt, angry, or defensive, his ears won't be as open. Not everyone is ready to talk all the time. Wait until you're both calm and focused. Also, don't force him to open up—that will just lead to another argument. Keep in mind that because you're such a big talker, your partner may not feel he's being heard and may not trust you to really listen. So be mindful of this when he *does* open up—and make a conscious effort to be a good listener. That means conveying that you hear and understand him (by asking questions to clarify and restating exactly what he said) and that you are not passing judgment.

(Mostly Ds)

## Exploder

When angered, you tend to lose control, often screaming or ranting and sometimes becoming verbally—even physically—abusive. In response, your mate either becomes a doormat or attacks back. In this adversarial atmosphere, no productive discussion occurs and your issue remains unresolved. And physical violence may result. If this is common in your household, you and your partner may need professional counseling to help calm your fighting style. You don't have to deny your true feelings to calm your couple conflicts. But if you want to preserve your relationship and have your needs met, you must convert raw rage into constructive communications. The next time you're angry, bite your tongue. Walk away, take five—or five thousand! Never allow yourself to react to a relationship problem impulsively. Focus on saving your marriage, not on winning the argument. You will need to develop an "observing ego," the part of the psyche that can step back and analyze your thoughts, feelings, and reactions. The more you exercise this part of your mind, the more "muscular" it becomes. In a short while, your observing ego will guide you to focus on whatever goal you set—in this case, making sure that you fight for the team, rather than on allowing your fury to take center stage.

Source: Jamie Turndorf, Ph.D., author of *Till Death Do Us Part (Unless I Kill You First)*

# Are You a Relationship Wimp?

A healthy—and long-lasting—love relationship requires a careful balancing of power. Are you a slave to a man's agenda? Or do you need help downsizing your own domineering personality? Take this quiz and find out if you're a relationship wimp—or a tyrant!

**1** Your significant other introduces you as a "friend" at a gathering. You

____ **a.** Diplomatically correct him and save the discussion for later

____ **b.** Smile and offer your hellos

____ **c.** Argue then and there, appearances be damned!

**2** The sex could be better, but you-know-who doesn't have a clue what to do. Your solution:

____ **a.** Fret silently after each feeble attempt—to the tune of his serious snores

____ **b.** Make an effort to gently guide your lover's hands to your secret pleasure zones

____ **c.** Have a breakfast briefing about the shortcomings between the sheets

**3** A lover promised to call at a certain time, but the phone is silent. You

____ **a.** Call immediately and remind him about his promise

____ **b.** Assume something important came up

____ **c.** Assume he doesn't care about you

**4** When it comes to making social plans, fulfilling family responsibilities, or doing household chores, your significant other knows he can count on you to

____ **a.** Put in extra hours doing the grunt work for both of you

____ **b.** Fulfill your fair share of your couple responsibilities—as long as he does the same

____ **c.** Instruct him on how such things are done

**5** When you're on the phone or out to eat, you

____ **a.** Always discuss your companion's life in detail

____ **b.** Tend to talk mostly about yourself

____ **c.** Discuss the topics that are affecting each of you

**6** What's your theory about apologizing after a relationship argument?

____ **a.** Just do it—you want to clear the air and move on, no matter who's to blame.

____ **b.** Don't do it—you're rarely wrong, so why should you apologize?

____ **c.** Be sincere—if you're wrong, you say so.

**7** The two of you are planning a small party for close friends. You'll mostly invite

____ **a.** An eclectic mix of people you both like

____ **b.** The girls from your yoga class, with their mates

____ **c.** His softball gang, with their mates

**8** You catch your man in a stupid lie (he went for a quick drink with his buddies instead of coming straight home, and then lied about it). You respond by

____ **a.** Threatening to call it quits unless he vows never, ever to lie to you again

____ **b.** Warning him that he better not ever lie to you again—you won't tolerate that kind of behavior

____ **c.** Pretending not to know about it

**9** Your mate refuses to spend a sunny Saturday with you and your mother (there's golfing/fishing/TV watching to be done). You

____ **a.** Sigh in resignation and start thinking of excuses to tell your mom

____ **b.** Express your unhappiness but understand his need for recreation, especially given the alternative

____ **c.** Find this unacceptable and demand an appearance, promising retribution if your demands are refused

**⑩ You've tried a new hairstyle and your man doesn't like it. In response you**

____ **a.** Argue the strong points of the new look

____ **b.** Give it two weeks and then decide for yourself

____ **c.** Hide under a hat until it grows out

**⑪ Who controls the remote (and your music and movie choices)?**

____ **a.** You haven't held the clicker in so long you forget what it looks like.

____ **b.** It can be a struggle, but you both get your turns.

____ **c.** You always decide what you'll both watch.

**⑫ Your most frequent style of couple communication is**

____ **a.** Expressing agreement—you to him

____ **b.** Nagging and lecturing—you at him

____ **c.** Engaging discussion—you and him

**⑬ You wish your love relationship were more intimate, so you**

____ **a.** Plan some time together and bring up your thoughts when the moment seems right

____ **b.** Accost your man at the door and let him have it for neglecting your emotional needs

____ **c.** Mope or complain to your friends

**⑭ How is the status of your relationship defined?**

____ **a.** You hope, with your fingers crossed, that your lover will tell you what you want to hear, but you're afraid to discuss it.

____ **b.** You'll bring it up if you have to; you need to know where you stand.

____ **c.** It's your way or the highway.

**⑮ You want to do something special this Saturday night with your man, so you**

____ **a.** Suggest a few options

____ **b.** Hope he'll plan a special night

____ **c.** Instruct your man to start planning

# Scoring

Give yourself the numerical value that matches each of your answers. Then add all 15 scores together and use your total score to find your result category.

1. a – 2  b – 1  c – 3
2. a – 1  b – 2  c – 3
3. a – 3  b – 2  c – 1
4. a – 1  b – 2  c – 3
5. a – 1  b – 3  c – 2
6. a – 1  b – 3  c – 2
7. a – 2  b – 3  c – 1
8. a – 3  b – 2  c – 1
9. a – 1  b – 2  c – 3
10. a – 3  b – 2  c – 1
11. a – 1  b – 2  c – 3
12. a – 1  b – 3  c – 2
13. a – 2  b – 3  c – 1
14. a – 1  b – 2  c – 3
15. a – 2  b – 1  c – 3

(35–45 points)

## The Bulldozer

You push and push to get your way in the name of love. While some may admire your focus and persistence, that's not the best behavior to establish a healthy, long-lasting relationship. Save the tough stuff for the conference room and stop trying to schedule, control, convince, and convert your man. Forced romantic involvement and the pressure to please turn off most men. They want some degree of control. Don't worry, there's plenty of power to go around. In the best relationships power is balanced. One day he's in the driver's seat; the next day, you are. So stop trying to steer your relationship all the time—let it plot its own course. You may be surprised to find that when you're not spending all of your time trying to control the relationship, you can actually relax and enjoy it.

(25–34 points)

## Ms. Even-Keel

You have a knack for forging great romantic relationships—balancing your own wants and desires with those of your partner. That doesn't mean you keep quiet when things are making you unhappy. You know when to accept another's weaknesses and when to draw the line at a person's disrespectful behavior. You aren't afraid to say what you want, like, or don't like. But you have a level-headed, fair-minded way of doing it; you don't rely on threats or overbearing behavior. You know that a happy, healthy relationship requires a balance of power and that a Queen of the Universe routine isn't going to fly. Besides, you don't need your man lapping at your feet like a puppy to feel confident and happy. You want a man who can hold up his end of an argument, express his opinions, and admit when he's wrong—just like you can.

### (15–24 points)

## Jellyfish

The man who snags you is one lucky guy . . . if he wants a puppet for a mate. Being the generous, agreeable soul may get you into heaven, but is it making you happy here on Earth? You don't have to transform yourself into a domineering diva, but you do need to get a little backbone and hold up your end of the relationship. Men (at least the desirable type) want a woman who has opinions and voices them, expresses her wants and needs, and doesn't let her guy get away with murder. So stop trying so hard to please and be yourself. If you want to see a certain movie on Saturday night, say so. Want him to visit your family with you more often? Speak up. One word of warning: If the man you're with has gotten used to your doormat status, he may be thrown by the new, more outspoken you. Either he'll love you more for it (a guy worth keeping) or feel threatened and insecure (a guy worth losing). If a breakup ensues, use this opportunity to seek a new relationship with someone who appreciates you for yourself.

# Can Your Relationship Survive the Long-Distance Test?

If you and your man live far apart or are considering a long-distance arrangement because of a new job or school, you're probably dying to know if your relationship can survive such a separation. Loving long-distance is certainly not easy, but some couples do make it work—and emerge stronger than ever. Answer these questions to find out if *your* relationship can go the distance.

**1** **Which statement best characterizes your relationship?**

____ **a.** You and your partner often argue about where things are headed.

____ **b.** You are both equally committed to making it work, and have similar feelings about where it is headed.

____ **c.** One of you is more committed to making it work than the other, but this hasn't posed a problem so far.

**2** **When one of you raises an issue you feel is important, the other person typically**

____ **a.** Is ready and willing to discuss it immediately

____ **b.** Asks if the issue can be discussed later

____ **c.** Gets annoyed or angry with the person for bringing it up

**3** **What role does sex play in your relationship?**

____ **a.** The sex is incredible. Chemistry is definitely one of the things that keeps you together.

____ **b.** Sex is not a very important part of your relationship.

____ **c.** Your relationship centers on many activities and experiences that you share—from sex to movies to travel.

**4** **If you had plans to see each other and one of you had to cancel, the other would**

____ **a.** Spend the time doing things the other would never want to do

____ **b.** Quickly make other plans with friends

____ **c.** Buy a pint of ice cream, rent some videos, and hang at home alone

**5** Which statement best describes the two of you?

____ **a.** You're both spontaneous people and you're always discovering new things together.

____ **b.** One of you is always trying new things and encouraging the other to do the same.

____ **c.** You've each figured out what you enjoy in life and you like to stick to doing those things.

**6** Can you imagine seeing other people romantically?

____ **a.** No way. You are completely happy with each other.

____ **b.** Probably not. One of you has brought up the idea in the past but the other wasn't comfortable with it.

____ **c.** Maybe. If you set ground rules at the outset and were both comfortable with them, it might work.

**7** Which statement is closest to the truth?

____ **a.** You have male friends and he has female friends, and you trust each other completely.

____ **b.** One or both of you has a tendency to get a little jealous when the other mentions friends of the opposite sex.

____ **c.** Jealousy (of opposite-sex as well as same-sex friends) and possessiveness are not foreign to your relationship.

**8** Do you and your partner have active social lives?

____ **a.** One of you has many friends; the other has almost no one else to spend time with.

____ **b.** You both have friends outside the relationship and often spend time with them.

____ **c.** The two of you are most interested in each other. You have some other acquaintances, but spend most of your time together.

# Scoring

Give yourself the numerical value that matches each of your answers. Then add all eight scores together and use your total score to find your result category.

1. **a** – 1   **b** – 3   **c** – 2
2. **a** – 3   **b** – 2   **c** – 1
3. **a** – 1   **b** – 2   **c** – 3
4. **a** – 2   **b** – 3   **c** – 1
5. **a** – 3   **b** – 2   **c** – 1
6. **a** – 1   **b** – 2   **c** – 3
7. **a** – 3   **b** – 2   **c** – 1
8. **a** – 2   **b** – 3   **c** – 1

(19–24 points)

## Distance Will Make Your Hearts Grow Fonder

Your relationship has what it takes to survive. If you're already living apart or foresee a geographical change in the near future, there's sure to be some genuine "I miss you," but you would cope by filling your life with friends and activities. You both understand that sitting at home alone moping won't help the situation, and could hurt your relationship. You know you both need to find meaning in your life to complement your relationship, no matter how much your partner means to you. Your relationship is already healthy in other ways: You're equally committed to making your relationship work; you're both comfortable and willing to discuss important issues; neither is averse to taking risks in your relationship, which means your relationship can evolve. You're also creating a solid trust, which will allow you to build independent social lives. Keep it up and you two are destined to live happily ever after—either long-distance or, hopefully, side-by-side.

(13–18 points)

## Distance May Distance You

Your quiz result is as ambiguous as your relationship: Your relationship may or may not survive separation. You'll probably come to realize how different the two of you are—in likes, dislikes, and how you feel about your relationship. While opposites can and do attract, opposites who live apart may just grow further apart—as the two of you fill your lives with other people and focus less on each other. Jealousy and temptation may prove too much for your already tenuous bond, given that one (or both) of you already questions the other's commitment or is interested in pursuing other romantic opportunities. If you want this relationship to have a fighting chance, work on some key areas: You both need to be equally committed; you need to communicate better (listen, talk through and resolve troubling issues, and so on); and you both need to be willing to take risks so your relationship can evolve as you both grow and change. Most important, you must establish a solid level of trust. Without that, your relationship won't survive even the Short-Distance Test.

## (8–12 points)
## Distance Will Open New Doors

Unfortunately, your relationship probably will not survive a separation. While most of the time you two appear happy as a couple, lack of a shared vision and poor communication plague your relationship. In addition, you lack other crucial qualities important for a successful long-distance relationship, such as a solid level of trust and coping strategies for being apart. You're so into being with each other that you've probably let your relationships with friends fall by the wayside. The result: too much time spent alone at home when the other is not around. For a long-distance relationship to thrive, both partners must have active lives with no attached feelings of jealousy, anger, or guilt. Both of you must also be willing to let your relationship evolve as your living situation changes— something neither of you seems willing to do. The good news is that since neither of you seems especially devoted to the relationship, a geographical separation may be just the impetus you need to end things amicably and pursue other romantic opportunities.

# 6

# Reveal Your Relationship with Friends and Family

**And learn more about them—and yourself!**

What Kind of Friend Are You?

Are You and Your Friend As Close As You Think?

What Does Your Relationship with Your Mother Say about You?

Is Sibling Rivalry Still Running Your Life?

# What Kind of Friend Are You?

We all have different ideas about what it means to be a friend. Some of us expect more than others, and some are willing to give more (time, support, and so on) to our friends. Take this quiz to find out what your friendship style is—and how similar it is to your friends'.

**❶ How easy is it for your friends to get in touch with you?**

____ **a.** Easy—they have your home phone, work phone, cell phone, and email.

____ **b.** Not so easy—they only have your email (those who are not Internet savvy have your work phone).

____ **c.** Easy enough—they have your work phone and email.

____ **d.** Extremely easy—they have your home phone, work phone, email, cell phone, and IM, and they know they can always come knocking on your door.

**❷ If you were planning your wedding today and could choose only two bridesmaids, could you do it?**

____ **a.** Sure, you'd ask your two best friends and be done with it.

____ **b.** It would be difficult—you have a lot of close friends; you wouldn't know how to choose just two without offending anyone.

____ **c.** If you had two siblings, sure, but you can't really think of two friends close enough to stand with you at the altar.

____ **d.** Probably not—your wedding would probably be so small and intimate, you can't imagine having a bridal party at all.

**❸ You call a friend just to say hello and get her answering machine. How long until you feel snubbed by her lack of response or wonder if she got the message?**

____ **a.** Up to a week—you're pretty flexible, but once a week has passed, you start to get annoyed.

____ **b.** Two or three days—even though life is hectic, it's important to touch base with friends.

____ **c.** One day—between friends, any longer than that is plain old rude.

____ **d.** You don't feel snubbed, but you don't wait for the phone to ring, either—you've got plenty of other friends.

**4** **To you, a friend is someone who knows your**

____ **a.** Full name

____ **b.** Favorite drink

____ **c.** Birthday

____ **d.** (Real) weight and your (real) bra size

**5** **At the last minute, your favorite man (husband/boyfriend/crush) suggests a romantic evening for two. But you have plans with a friend. What do you do?**

____ **a.** Do a bit of cost-benefit analysis (is the benefit of accepting the "date" going to cost you too much in friendship?).

____ **b.** Ask for a rain check from Mr. Wonderful—romance or not, friends come first.

____ **c.** Reschedule with the friend—period.

____ **d.** Ask your friend (somewhat sheepishly) if you can reschedule and promise to make it up to her—you'd do the same for her in a second.

**6** **If a friend were throwing you a birthday party, she'd do the right thing by**

____ **a.** Getting your favorite people together at your favorite place for your favorite meal. She knows what you like and she'd be sure to make your day special.

____ **b.** Inviting just a handful of really close friends for an intimate evening of girl talk.

____ **c.** Gathering a group together for dinner out—she knows you'd enjoy a casual outing with some friendly faces.

____ **d.** Inviting everyone and anyone you know, plus plenty of new faces—she knows you love to meet and greet.

**7** **Your close friends are those with whom you**

____ **a.** Do regular activities

____ **b.** Feel comfortable sharing personal stories

____ **c.** Can share your deepest feelings, darkest thoughts, and secrets

____ **d.** You don't really have any close friends

**8** **What would you be upset with a friend for *not* sharing with you?**

____ **a.** Not much—you don't expect your friends to tell you everything about themselves.

____ **b.** Something important, like a great first date, a career-boosting meeting, or an ill child.

____ **c.** A major problem, such as a health concern for her or a family member.

____ **d.** Not sharing? You tell each other everything!

# Scoring

Give yourself the numerical value that matches each of your answers. Then add all eight scores together and use your total score to find your result category.

1. a – 3   b – 1   c – 2   d – 4
2. a – 4   b – 3   c – 2   d – 1
3. a – 2   b – 3   c – 4   d – 1
4. a – 1   b – 2   c – 3   d – 4
5. a – 3   b – 4   c – 1   d – 2
6. a – 4   b – 3   c – 2   d – 1
7. a – 2   b – 3   c – 4   d – 1
8. a – 1   b – 3   c – 2   d – 4

(26–32 points)
## You Are a Best Friend

You flourish in close, intimate friendships; cherish your closest friends; and spend most of your "friend" time with them. Casual friends and acquaintances are of little importance to you. You make friends for life, and tend to look at your friends as your family. You are a giving, loyal, and trustworthy friend and you expect the same in return. While this approach to friendship may work when you are joined with another Best Friend type, your expectations lean toward the unrealistic. You should be able to depend on your friends but be independent from them and have them be independent from you. Friendships should involve fun as well as close connection and problem solving. If you can't lighten up and laugh together, you're missing one of the greatest joys of friendship!

(20–25 points)
## You Are a Close Friend

You are a faithful friend: loyal, trustworthy, and generous, with realistic expectations. You understand your obligations to your friends—to listen, support, advise when necessary and so on—but you don't take too much responsibility for their feelings and needs. You love that your closest friends know personal details and crazy quirks about you, and you love knowing these types of things about them. While you're comfortable being close, you don't feel the need to share every intimate detail with your friends and you appreciate time away from them.

## (14–19 points)
## You Are a Casual Friend

Your friendship Rolodex is filled with work friends, gym friends, and friends you see at regular activities, such as pottery class, Mommy & Me, or yoga. You know you'll see them regularly, so you don't usually feel the need to take your relationship out of that context. Taking these friendships to the next level is not on your agenda—most likely because your life is so busy you simply don't have the time to devote to developing close friendships. Likewise, it's a good bet that your busy life includes a romantic partner, children, or a close extended family. No matter how busy you are,

remember that friendship can make you happier and healthier, and even enhance your marriage or partnership. And friendship, like love, requires an investment of time and effort.

## (8–13 points)
## You Are an Acquaintance

Your motto is "the more, the merrier," and what better way to fill your life with lots of different friends than by keeping your schedule loose and your options open? While you're a fun and interesting friend, your independence may get in the way of true friendship. Balancing a friend's needs with your own is crucial to friendship success. While it's okay to miss a friend's party because you are out of town on business or scheduled vacation before you knew about her big bash, running off for a weekend of fun when your friend is counting on you to help with something important isn't going to cut it. Close friendships involve some degree of interdependence, when both friends are influenced by the plans and decisions of the other.

# Are You and Your Friend as Close as You Think?

It's not uncommon for friends to have different opinions about the closeness of their relationship. Take this test to find out how close you *really* are with your friends—and what you can do to build stronger bonds in the future.

**❶ When a friend does something to upset you, you usually**

____ **a.** Want to hear her side of the story

____ **b.** Want to tell her how to make the situation better

____ **c.** Come right out and tell her what she did wrong

____ **d.** Keep it to yourself

**❷ A friend calls to talk about sex— specifically about her sorry experiences in the sack the night before. You react by**

____ **a.** Asking for all the details

____ **b.** Offering the tip you remember from that risqué magazine article you read

____ **c.** Sympathizing and offering a few intimate stories of your own—maybe even a few you've heard from other friends

____ **d.** Sympathizing without offering details, stories, or tips; there is such a thing as too much information!

**❸ If asked to pin a professional label on you, your friends would say you would make a great**

____ **a.** Bartender—you're such a sympathetic listener

____ **b.** Advice columnist—you'd give Dear Abby a run for her money

____ **c.** Talk-show host—you know how to get people gabbing and could fill dead air time in a snap

____ **d.** Novelist—they know you relish your own schedule, space, and alone time

**❹ How many people know about your first love/worst breakup story/most embarrassing romantic moment?**

___ **a.** Only your best friend and your mom.

___ **b.** Most of your friends know, but their stories are worse!

___ **c.** At this point it's pretty much common knowledge; besides, it's a hilarious story!

___ **d.** No one! (Besides the other person who was involved.)

**5** Over eggs Benedict and Bloody Marys with a friend in crisis, you concentrate on

___ **a.** Hearing her out

___ **b.** Solving her problem

___ **b.** Cheering her up

___ **d.** Your food

**6** If a TV character in an office sitcom were based on you, how would you complete this description? She's the coworker who

___ **a.** Everyone tells gossip and stories to

___ **b.** Everyone goes to for career guidance

___ **c.** Is the source for gossip and stories

___ **d.** Pretty much keeps to herself

**7** When you're in a bad mood, you like to

___ **a.** Hear someone else's sob story—it takes your mind off your own problems

___ **b.** Focus on helping someone else solve her problems—you enjoy feeling useful

___ **c.** Vent—to as many people as will listen

___ **d.** Take your phone off the hook—you just want to be left alone

**8** When it's time to celebrate your birthday, you usually

___ **a.** Ask a friend or your significant other to do your favorite activity with you—it's the one day when you do the inviting, instead of the other way around

___ **b.** Call your closest friends and family and invite them over for an evening of good conversation and good food

___ **c.** Whip up an email invitation and send it to as many people as you can think of—what could be better than a big, loud, fun party with you as hostess?

___ **d.** Keep it quiet—it's your day to spend the way you want

# Scoring

Add up the number of As, Bs, Cs, and Ds you chose. Find the category in which you had the most responses. This category explains your style of communication when it comes to friendship—and what that means for your closeness level.

## (Mostly As)
### You Are a Listener

One of the best ways to be a close friend is by being a good listener. But while friends cherish your nurturing ways and willingness to always lend an ear, you don't always love to share your own stories with them. That may be an obstacle when it comes to developing honest, deep, and fulfilling friendships: You may not be as close with your friends as you might think. Keep in mind that sharing feelings, life experiences, and personal information is a basic feature of friendship. If someone shares with you and you never do, you're weakening the relationship—no matter how good a listener you are.

## (Mostly Bs)
### You Are a Reliable Advisor

You love to give good advice and your friends usually love to receive it. You have a way of making your friends feel cared for, and that's surely one reason why you feel so close. But be careful: While you have the best interests of your friends at heart, you run the risk of offering too much judgment (which can be viewed as criticism) and too little unconditional love and acceptance. Sure, your friends may say that they want your good advice, but the honest truth may not really be what they're after. Deep down what most friends want is unconditional acceptance. Try to look at the situation from your friend's side, not from your own viewpoint. And offer input in the most positive way possible. Remember that you can't always be the one to solve problems, so it's important to develop your listening and sharing skills to be an all-around good friend.

## (Mostly Cs)
### You Are a Chatterbox

You love to communicate and converse, and you know how to use discussion to motivate a crowd of pals, cheer up a girlfriend, and even charm prospective friends. You're the bright spark everyone loves to be near, and that's what makes your friendships feel so close. That said, you may sometimes *think* a friendship is closer than it is, just because you've spent so much time talking to someone. To develop a truly close friendship, you have to put in equal amounts of *listening* time, so you can really get to know each other. Another thing to watch out for: Don't let your excitement over a good story get the better of you—what a friend tells you in confidence should remain between the two of you.

(Mostly Ds)
## You Are a Private Person

You're not comfortable sharing all of your deepest thoughts and feelings, no matter how much you like your friends. While friends should respect each other's privacy, sharing feelings, life experiences, and personal information is a basic feature of friendship. If someone confides in you and you never confide in her, your friendship will never develop into an honest and fulfilling bond. Work on opening up more if you want to get truly close to your friends.

# What Does Your Relationship with Your Mother Say about You?

Whether your relationship with your mother is close or distant, the way you relate to her says a lot about the kind of woman you are today, and who you're going to become. Discover your true mother-daughter relationship—and what that says about your personality—by taking this quiz.

**1** When it comes to spending time with other women, you find it

____ **a.** Pretty hard to reveal yourself

____ **b.** Easy to be yourself

____ **c.** Easiest to loosen up around close friends

**2** As a child, you were closer to your

____ **a.** Mother

____ **b.** Father or sibling

____ **c.** You weren't close to any immediate members of the family

**3** Your general outlook is that

____ **a.** Life has its ups and downs

____ **b.** Life is tough

____ **c.** The world is a caring place

**4** When your mother does special things for you, you feel

____ **a.** Cared for

____ **b.** A little uncomfortable

____ **c.** Annoyed

**5** When you have a problem, you usually

____ **a.** Ask for help if you really need it

____ **b.** Get help immediately

____ **c.** Work it out yourself

**6** When it comes to spending time with your mother, you

____ **a.** Wish that you enjoyed it more

____ **b.** Feel like you should try to be more available for her

____ **c.** Think that you are together a lot—maybe too much

**7** **When it comes to trusting other people, you**

____ **a.** Automatically assume the best of them

____ **b.** Give them the benefit of the doubt

____ **c.** Make them earn your trust

**8** **You think of your mother as a**

____ **a.** Person with her own problems

____ **b.** Saint, in her own special way

____ **c.** Woman you admire but don't always get along with

**9** **During holidays, it's important to you to**

____ **a.** Call your mother

____ **b.** Be with your mother

____ **c.** Have some time alone

**10** **When your mother asks you for a favor, you**

____ **a.** Try your best to help

____ **b.** Have to check your schedule

____ **c.** Do it without thinking

**11** **You and your mother talk on the phone, email, or meet in person**

____ **a.** More than twice a week

____ **b.** Once every couple of weeks or less

____ **c.** Only on special occasions

**12** **You think your childhood was**

____ **a.** Kind of tough and problematic

____ **b.** Pretty average

____ **c.** Really good, almost idyllic

**13** **When you have a problem you need to talk about, you call**

____ **a.** Your mother

____ **b.** Your friends

____ **c.** Anyone but your mother

**14** **People would describe you as**

____ **a.** Independent

____ **b.** Nurturing

____ **c.** Sometimes distant

**15** **When it comes to discussing your friends and relationships, you**

____ **a.** Don't talk about them with your mother

____ **b.** Give your mother every detail

____ **c.** Generally tell your mother something about them

# Scoring

Give yourself the numerical value that matches each of your answers. Then add all 15 scores together and use your total score to find your result category.

1. a – 1  b – 3  c – 2
2. a – 3  b – 2  c – 1
3. a – 2  b – 1  c – 3
4. a – 3  b – 2  c – 1
5. a – 2  b – 3  c – 1
6. a – 1  b – 2  c – 3
7. a – 3  b – 2  c – 1
8. a – 1  b – 3  c – 2
9. a – 2  b – 3  c – 1
10. a – 2  b – 1  c – 3
11. a – 3  b – 2  c – 1
12. a – 1  b – 2  c – 3
13. a – 3  b – 2  c – 1
14. a – 2  b – 3  c – 1
15. a – 1  b – 3  c – 2

(36–45 points)
## Mother's Daughter

You are trusting, sentimental, and very close to your mother. She has played a positive role in your life, and that in turn allows you to play a positive role in other people's lives. Your mother has shaped your feminine identity in a major way, and your friends are sure to appreciate your nurturing quality. While you tend to be the caregiver in romantic relationships, the right man for you is the one who will also appreciate the part of you that likes to be taken care of. Even though you are very close to your mother, it's okay for you to separate and become independent. On a similar note, you may need to learn to see your mother as a person in her own right, rather than simply as a mother figure. The more you can understand what her life has really been like, the more you'll discover about her and the better you'll know her. This will allow your closeness to continue through the years.

(25–35 points)
## Dutiful Daughter

Your relationship with your mother is fairly smooth and comfortable. You admire her, stay in touch regularly, and appreciate her help when you need it. But you probably see your own life as very different from hers. And it is. But your mother has played a fairly positive role in your life and helped form your feminine identity. You understand that life has its ups and downs, and you feel comfortable when people want to help you through the lower points. That ability to feel nurtured is key to the ability to be nurturing to other people. Because your mother is a powerful presence in your life, you may at times wish that you had more distance: Your relationship can get stormy. But those moments are a natural part of separating and establishing your own identity at any age. It's important to know that two people can be separate and still love and cherish each other.

## (15–24 points)
## Do-It-Yourself Child

You are a self-sufficient woman who knows how to take care of herself. You don't expect other people to take care of you, but remember that vulnerability is an important part of intimacy. And this is true for any relationship, whether it's friendship, family, or romance. You probably see your life as very different from your mother's. You don't understand other women who go on and on about their mothers, and you are probably suspicious of a man who is overly attached to his. This distance is healthy when it comes to separating and establishing your own identity. But if you want to improve your relationship with your mother (or change how you feel and think about her), try looking at her as a woman with a life and feelings of her own. If you can understand what her life has been like and how different it is from yours, you may become more empathetic. Try to learn more about your mother. Not only will it give you something to talk about, it will help you understand and discover more about the woman you are.

# Is Sibling Rivalry Still Running Your Life?

When you were a kid and your sibling got a bigger, better new toy, you cried your eyes out. The question is, are you still caught up in sibling rivalry or have you grown up and moved on? Take this test and find out the truth.

**1** **Looking back on your childhood, you feel that your parents**

____ **a.** Always paid more attention to your sibling

____ **b.** Clearly loved you but could have paid a tad more attention

____ **c.** Always paid attention to you and gave you plenty of love

**2** **These days, when you and your sibling go home for the holidays**

____ **a.** You trade gifts and celebrate as one big, happy family

____ **b.** You get along well, but still bicker like kids over what to do and what to eat

____ **c.** You silently compete over whose gift your parents will like the most

**3** **If your sibling bought the latest flashy new stereo, you would probably**

____ **a.** Look at your stereo and feel a pang of jealousy

____ **b.** Buy your sibling some new CDs to play on it

____ **c.** Go out and buy a pricier, flashier stereo

**4** **The last time your sibling got a promotion at work, you**

____ **a.** Felt like a total failure and vowed to start going into work an hour earlier

____ **b.** Took your phone off the hook, in case your sibling called to brag

____ **c.** Took your sibling out to celebrate or called to offer sincere congratulations

**5** **The last time you and your sibling got into an argument was**

____ **a.** So long ago you can't remember

____ **b.** This week, and you're still fuming

____ **c.** A few months ago

**6** If you were to meet your sibling for a friendly game of tennis, you would most likely

____ **a.** Not keep track of points and just have a good time

____ **b.** Play competitively like you always do, but then go out for a drink afterward

____ **c.** Fight over every line call, and leave not on speaking terms

**7** When people ask you what's new with your sibling, you

____ **a.** Smile and say nice things, but secretly wish you could disclose the latest dirty gossip

____ **b.** Share the latest dirty gossip

____ **c.** Rave about how great she or he is doing, no matter what

**8** If you were to lose your job, you would probably

____ **a.** Feel embarrassed to tell your sibling

____ **b.** Call your sibling right away to get advice and support

____ **c.** Keep it from your sibling for as long as possible

**9** If you badly needed a loan, you would

____ **a.** Feel comfortable borrowing money from your sibling

____ **b.** Borrow money from your sibling only as a last resort

____ **c.** Sooner become a bum on the street than admit to your sibling that your funds were low

# Scoring

Give yourself the numerical value that matches each of your answers. Then add all nine scores together and use your total score to find your result category.

1. **a** – 3  **b** – 2  **c** – 1
2. **a** – 1  **b** – 2  **c** – 3
3. **a** – 2  **b** – 1  **c** – 3
4. **a** – 3  **b** – 2  **c** – 1
5. **a** – 1  **b** – 3  **c** – 2
6. **a** – 1  **b** – 2  **c** – 3
7. **a** – 2  **b** – 3  **c** – 1
8. **a** – 2  **b** – 1  **c** – 3
9. **a** – 1  **b** – 2  **c** – 3

**(22–27 points)**
## Permanent Competitor

Not only is your competitive nature in danger of ruining your relationship with your sibling (or what's left of it), you're wasting energy that could be channeled into making a healthier, happier life for yourself. If you have children, you might also want to consider what kind of an example you're setting for them. It's time for you to deal with and finally get over your feelings about your childhood, and leave issues from those early years where they belong—in the past.

**(15–21 points)**
## Quiet Competitor

Although you don't seem to be extremely competitive with your sibling, you do have a latent competitive streak, so be careful. Try to leave issues from childhood where they belong—in the past. If you allow a competitive spirit to run your family life, you'll only hurt yourself. You don't want to risk ruining your sibling relationship for good, and if you have children, you don't want to set a bad example for them.

**(9–14 points)**
## Model Sibling

Your parents must have raised you well. You seem comfortable with yourself and don't feel the need to compete with others to validate your own life. Your noncompetitive attitude about family allows you and your sibling to enjoy a peaceful, nurturing relationship. Whatever sibling rivalry existed during your growing up years is well behind you. Now you're happy to be living your own life, with your sibling as a welcome part of it.

# 7

# Bring Out Your Best Look

## And be the most beautiful you can be!

How Alluring Are You?

Are You a Beauty Master—or Disaster?

The Fashion Test: What's Your Style?

Are You a Beauty Product Junkie?

What Lipstick Color Are You?

What Fragrance Is Right for You?

Do You Need a Makeover?

# How Alluring Are You?

Your look and style—as well as your inner beauty—are the essential ingredients of your allure. Take this quiz to find out how alluring you are and the impression you're making on others.

**1** **Your "knock-out" outfit is**

____ **a.** Tailored

____ **b.** Snug

____ **c.** Tight

**2** **Do you wear accessories in your hair?**

____ **a.** Sometimes—for a favorite look or on hectic mornings.

____ **b.** Rarely, if ever—unless a scrunchie or headband during face washing counts.

____ **c.** Often—you like to know every strand is in place.

**3** **The allure of your signature makeup look lies in emphasizing your**

____ **a.** Radiant skin—where natural beauty begins

____ **b.** Luscious lips—the better to kiss him with

____ **c.** Expressive eyes—they're the windows to the soul

**4** **Finish the following sentence with the statement that's most like you. Your hair is**

____ **a.** One of your best features. Mostly you wear it naturally; you don't like it to be too "done." You don't even like to blow-dry it too often, to keep it healthy.

____ **b.** Always styled. You love product! And you're religious about keeping your hairstyle fashionable and sexy.

____ **c.** Perfect for your face, shape, and style. Your stylist tweaks it to keep up with trends, but you've found a look that works—and you work it.

**5** **When you're in his arms, you feel sexiest in**

____ **a.** A lavender-scented bubble bath

____ **b.** A sleeping bag under a starry sky

____ **c.** Red satin sheets and candlelight

**6** You're out on the town when you see The One That Got Away across the room. You

____ **a.** Catch his eye and wave him over. If it had been meant to be, you'd still be together. But you might as well be friendly.

____ **b.** Walk up and say hello—and find out whether he's seeing anyone now. Regardless, you make sure he sees how much more luscious you've become so he can eat his heart out.

____ **c.** Smile if he catches your eye, but if there's a move to be made, it's his. You're curious, but you've never chased a man—and aren't going to start now.

**7** You get a $200 gift certificate to your favorite spa. You can't wait to be pampered with

____ **a.** The ultrafacial—exfoliating, extraction, light peel, the works. Nothing feels more purifying and rejuvenating.

____ **b.** A full waxing—brows, legs, bikini. Nothing is better than that smooth-as-silk feeling—and you might as well pamper your man, too!

____ **c.** A 90-minute Swedish massage. Other than great sex, what's more sensuous?

## Scoring

Give yourself the numerical value that matches each of your answers. Then add all seven scores together and use your total score to find your result category.

1. a – 1   b – 2   c – 3
2. a – 2   b – 3   c – 1
3. a – 1   b – 3   c – 2
4. a – 2   b – 3   c – 1
5. a – 1   b – 2   c – 3
6. a – 2   b – 3   c – 1
7. a – 3   b – 1   c – 2

(17–21 points)
### Va-Va-Voom Vixen

Your allure is all about possibility and passion. Your ever-glossed lips, gorgeous mane, and sensuous approach to life send a provocative, powerful message to the objects of your desire: You're here, you're in love with life—and you're ready for anything! When it comes to fashion, if your clothing isn't body conscious, it's not for you. When it comes to attitude, your motto is, "If I don't ask for what I want, how can I be sure I'll get it?" And as for beauty, you've always believed lovely is good, but luscious is better! Your siren's heart and lush approach to beauty draw men to you like bees to honey.

## (12–16 points)
### Earth Angel

Your allure is all about earthy sensuality. Your natural beauty, glowing skin, and warm nature send a soulful message to the objects of your desire: Only authentic hearts need apply! You love clothing in natural fabrics that make you feel good. You often have a sense that you're in tune—with your friends and with your surroundings. You've always taken great care with your appearance, because you never feel more right than when you reveal your best self to the world. Your allure is like a mesmerizing fire, drawing men to you who seek warmth, comfort—and heat!

## (7–11 points)
### Demure Darling

Your allure is all about your mystery. To anyone who's really looking, it's obvious that your sometimes reserved exterior barely holds back your strong, deeply romantic heart and passionate soul. Your Grace Kelly-like fashion style (classics, luxurious fabrics, jet-set casual) makes women want to wear your clothes—and makes men want to peel them off. You prize intellect as much as you do passion. Your approach to beauty is to make it seem effortless, but you have been religiously moisturizing your hands, face, and neck since you can remember. Men are drawn to you for your classy air, but stay to unravel your straight-laced loveliness and reveal the sultry sylph within.

# Are You a Beauty Master—or Disaster?

Do you know the tricks of the beauty trade that can have you looking gorgeous in mere minutes? Test your talents with this quiz—and learn how to become a beauty whiz in no time!

**1** **Which of the following can be used to treat cellulite?**

____ **a.** Coffee grounds

____ **b.** Catsup

____ **c.** Apple juice

**2** **When you choose a new eye shadow, you**

____ **a.** Match your eye color

____ **b.** Choose an understated and neutral shade

____ **c.** Go for a sparkly shade worn by your favorite star

**3** **When you wake up with puffy eyes, you do what the pros do and**

____ **a.** Reach for your concealer

____ **b.** Take a baby's teething ring from the freezer where you stored it for this emergency

____ **c.** Apply a small amount of hemorrhoid cream to the area

**4** **If your hair is "tapered" it means**

____ **a.** Your hair gradually slants from short to long

____ **b.** You have a style with bangs

____ **c.** It needs to be shampooed

**5** **Your nails are discolored from nail polish. To get the yellow out, you**

____ **a.** Cover them immediately with dark red polish

____ **b.** Apply hydrogen peroxide or bleach and let it sit for three minutes

____ **c.** Soak them in nail polish remover

**6** **You're on a trip and wake up with a zit and no zapper. In a pinch, you cover the blemish with**

____ **a.** Vaseline

____ **b.** Toothpaste

____ **c.** Toner

**7** Your hair is gunky from too many styling products. To get rid of the build-up, you rinse with

____ **a.** Apple cider vinegar

____ **b.** Honey

____ **c.** Vodka

**8** What should you do to your skin before applying a self-tanner?

____ **a.** Apply sunscreen

____ **b.** Moisturize

____ **c.** Exfoliate

**9** All the pros now apply foundation using

____ **a.** A washcloth

____ **b.** A brush

____ **c.** Fingers

## Scoring

Give yourself the numerical value that matches each of your answers. Then add all nine scores together and use your total score to find your result category.

1. a – 3 b – 1 c – 2
2. a – 1 b – 3 c – 2
3. a – 1 b – 2 c – 3
4. a – 3 b – 2 c – 1
5. a – 2 b – 3 c – 1
6. a – 1 b – 3 c – 2
7. a – 3 b – 1 c – 2
8. a – 1 b – 2 c – 3
9. a – 1 b – 3 c – 2

(22–27 points)
## Beauty Whiz

You have a distinct makeup look and know how to achieve it. You don't need advice (you have it down already), but you love to hear about the latest products and like to be the first among your friends to discover new ones. You're into trends and wear them well, and are fashion forward in every aspect of your beauty style and preferences. This makes you a sought-after beauty resource for your friends. The added allure of your personal style is that no matter how hard you work to create your look, it appears effortless—a myth you're careful to maintain. For example, you wouldn't be caught dead by anyone—especially a man—retouching your lipstick in public (let other women get caught primping!). Whether you're getting ready for a glamorous evening or going casual, you know how to master any look and present yourself perfectly at all times.

(15–21 points)

## Beauty Student

You're well on your way to becoming a master of all things beauty, but you're not quite there yet. Sometimes it's easy to look at ever-fashionable friends and glossy magazines and feel that practically every woman but you has pulled together her own signature style. Take heart! More important, give yourself a break. Finding the hairstyles and makeup looks that work best for you is a continually evolving process. The next time you're looking through a beauty magazine, try this reality-based trick: Notice what you're drawn to (say, Angelina Jolie's lips). But this time, trade the impossible-to-achieve ("I want plump lips like hers") for the easy-to-do ("I'm going to make my lips look nude, soft, and glistening, too"). The first and last rule of mastering your beauty style is to choose a look you like and then *adapt the look you love to work for you.*

(9–14 points)

## Beauty Beginner

You have an exquisite sense of freedom that comes from not giving a hoot about the latest beauty trends! Those who think of you as a beauty disaster just don't appreciate that you're a woman with her own personal—and often natural—style. While some people find makeup techniques fun to learn, you can't be bothered. Your carefree makeup attitude allows you to fully enjoy your mornings (you can sleep late or get in a good workout) and evenings (you can be ready for just about anything in record time). A special bonus: Your low-maintenance routine is definitely appreciated by the men in your life, who love your natural look and fuss-free ways.

# The Fashion Test: What's Your Style?

Style is a reflection of personality. What does *your* style reveal about the inner you, and what does your personality say your style should be? Discover your true style—and your best look—by taking this test. Plus, find out your celebrity style role models!

**1** Your favorite decade is

____ **a.** 2000s

____ **b.** 1940s

____ **c.** 1970s

____ **d.** 1890s

____ **e.** 1990s

____ **f.** 2010s

**2** Your feel-good clothing item is

____ **a.** An old pair of jeans

____ **b.** A camel hair coat

____ **c.** A sexy slip dress

____ **d.** Cashmere socks

____ **e.** A vintage blouse

____ **f.** A deconstructed jacket

**3** The music that moves you most is

____ **a.** Pop

____ **b.** Broadway scores

____ **c.** Disco

____ **d.** Classic rock

____ **e.** Classical

____ **f.** Electronica

**4** Your dream home is

____ **a.** A ski house in Aspen

____ **b.** A penthouse in a fancy New York City neighborhood

____ **c.** A city loft in a cool, arty area

____ **d.** A country farmhouse

____ **e.** A Victorian mansion

____ **f.** Anything designed by Rem Koolhaas, the award-winning, unconventional architect

**5** On your ideal vacation, you

____ **a.** Backpack through Europe

____ **b.** Jet to Paris

____ **c.** Head for the hottest spa

____ **d.** Go on safari

____ **e.** Hole up in a bed-and-breakfast

____ **f.** Snowboard

**6** Your lingerie drawer is overflowing with

____ **a.** Sport bras and breathable micro fibers

____ **b.** Designer labels

____ **c.** Navy or taupe silk

____ **d.** Cotton

____ **e.** Frills, lace, and bows

____ **f.** Thongs

**7** You mostly read

____ **a.** Maps

____ **b.** Novels

____ **c.** Fashion magazines

____ **d.** Newspapers

____ **e.** Poetry

____ **f.** Webzines

**8** You love, love, love to wear

____ **a.** Fleece

____ **b.** Cashmere

____ **c.** Leather

____ **d.** Denim

____ **e.** Lace

____ **f.** Rubber

**9** If you were a dog, you'd be a

____ **a.** Greyhound

____ **b.** Shih Tzu

____ **c.** Weimaraner

____ **d.** Mutt

____ **e.** Irish setter

____ **f.** Chihuahua

**10** When you're at a bar and he says, "What can I get you?" you say

____ **a.** Orange juice, on the rocks

____ **b.** Gin and tonic

____ **c.** Cosmopolitan

____ **d.** White wine spritzer

____ **e.** Red wine

____ **f.** Martini, extra dry, with an olive

**11** Your must-have beauty item is

____ **a.** Chap Stick

____ **b.** Red lipstick

____ **c.** Liquid eyeliner

____ **d.** Moisturizer

____ **e.** Perfume

____ **f.** Glitter

## Scoring

Add up the number of As, Bs, Cs, Ds, Es, and Fs you chose. Find the category in which you had the most responses to determine your style—and what that reveals about the inner you.

## (Mostly As)
## Athletic Style

You love the outdoors, and being fashionable is not necessarily at the top of your mind. For you, clothing and makeup must be utilitarian and can't slow you down or perish if exposed to a dose of sweat. You often favor body-conscious clothing because it shows off the figure you've achieved, but you never wear anything that inhibits movement. Clothes often look sexier on you because you are so comfortable in your own skin. The fabrics you choose to put next to your skin have to breathe, and your makeup is usually minimal. You generally keep your hair away from your face, and you're one of those women who, when they let their tresses down and put on some lipstick, people really notice. Your style role models include Sandra Bullock, Gabrielle Reese, and Venus Williams.

## (Mostly Bs)
## Classic Style

Elegance and sophistication are your bywords. Sometimes you are downright glamorous, but your innate fashion sense is drawn to quality and timelessness. You buy items that will always look stylish because, while they may not come from the top designers, they will always reflect current styles. Everything you wear is well made. Appropriateness is crucial to you because fashion is about poise. You are very attuned to what's flattering, and grooming is important—no doubt you don't chew gum in public, have good posture, and write thank-you notes quickly. You are, at heart, a traditionalist. Your style role models include Gwyneth Paltrow, Halle Berry, and Grace Kelly.

## (Mostly Cs)
## Fashion Forward

Trends are important to you. You are actively engaged in reports from the runway and pay attention to the subtlest changes in the look of the moment. It is critical that what you do and what you wear be up-to-the-minute and just ahead of the curve—you're always the first of your friends to try a new look or buy the latest fashion item. This means that your hair, makeup, and clothes are constantly changing. Fashion is obviously a large part of your identity, and it will always hold a distinct place in your life. Your style is about status and showing you're in the know. You could never be seriously involved with anyone who didn't have some appreciation of style. No doubt you're intuitive and work in a creative field. Your style role models include Sarah Jessica Parker, Madonna, and Drew Barrymore.

## (Mostly Ds)
## Natural Style

Style for you is almost accidental, but you usually have it because you have an eye for simplicity, good design, and fine materials. You like comfort, ease, and clothing that is made well. You will never be upstaged by an outfit; clothing is all about accenting whatever assets you naturally have. Likewise, your makeup and hair are usually understated and do not call attention. You like muted, earthy colors, and to wear your clothes a little bigger than your actual size. Fashion is not the first order of business in your life, so you lean toward simple lines and few accessories. You have several favorite items, and they tend to last forever. Much of your wardrobe is like an old, reliable friend. Your style role models include Meg Ryan, Robin Wright Penn, and Helen Hunt.

## (Mostly Es)
## Romantic Style

Things aren't worth much to you unless they have some personal meaning or a foothold in the past. You gravitate toward vintage clothing and jewelry. For you, objects have a past and a spirit that they carry with them. When it comes to fashion, you are very sensual and feminine, and how things feel is as important to you as how they look. You dress with your heart. You are not particularly interested in the style *du jour* because your reference points are timeless. When you think of trends, you tend to think in terms of century rather than season. You often have a signature color or hairstyle that you are very loyal to and perhaps known for. You are a dreamer, and you often think of clothing as costume. Your style role models include Winona Ryder, Diane Keaton, and Helena Bonham Carter.

## (Mostly Fs)
## Urban Chic

You love anything and everything representative of the new millennium. You believe in fashion that shocks, makeup that pushes the envelope, and hairstyles that are risky. You like people to react to how you look and live. You are drawn to new fabrics; unique silhouettes; and strong, unusual colors. You are spontaneous and creative, and are always responding to what's new. Trends are not your thing; you are *in* style, but only in the most out-there way. Much like Madonna in her early years, style for you is about challenging people and their notions of how things ought to be. Your style role models include Gwen Stefani, L'il Kim, and Rachel Leigh Cook.

# Are You a Beauty Product Junkie?

We all have our shopping addictions—handbags, shoes, jewelry. But for some of us, these are second to the experience of finding the perfect beauty product. Does an ad for a brand-new lipstick make your heart beat faster? Or are you the kind of product user who can pass on a sale for shampoo if you're already stocked? Exactly how much of a product junkie are you? Answer these questions and find out!

**1** **You shop for beauty products**

___ **a.** Daily

___ **b.** Once or twice a week

___ **c.** Once a month

**2** **You walk up to a swanky makeup counter and the salesperson greets you with**

___ **a.** "How may I help you?"

___ **b.** "Hello, how've you been?"

___ **c.** "The new colors came in this morning and I knew you'd want to be the first to try them."

**3** **You have a big date coming up. Is it time for a new lip color?**

___ **a.** Maybe—you did see an ad for a brand-new kiss-proof lip gloss.

___ **b.** Nah—you'll just wear what you always wear.

___ **c.** Of course—you've got to get one that'll go with your new dress.

**4** **You're at the mall on a mission to get your man a birthday present when you notice it's GWP time at your favorite makeup counter. You**

___ **a.** Wonder what GWP is

___ **b.** Make a beeline straight to the counter—miss out on GWP? Are you nuts?

___ **c.** Reluctantly keep walking—you've got to get to the men's department before closing

**5** How many beauty products in your possession have gone unused in the past year?

____ **a.** Five or more—you'll throw out something only if it starts to leak or smell.

____ **b.** One or more—you're holding onto it for a special occasion, like a New Year's Eve party.

____ **c.** None—why on earth would you keep something around that you don't use regularly?

**6** Does buying a new product give you a buzz?

____ **a.** No way—that's what Starbucks is for.

____ **b.** Sometimes—if you find a favorite at a really great price.

____ **c.** Most definitely—it's better than a first kiss!

**7** You're out on the town and decided to travel light with your keys, credit card, and lip gloss in a jacket pocket. On the dance floor, you realize you've dropped your lip gloss. You

____ **a.** Ask your girlfriend if you can borrow hers

____ **b.** Wet your lips with a cocktail and keep up the revelry

____ **c.** Get down on your hands and knees and search, search, search!

**8** Your best friend calls with a disturbing dilemma: She has a major zit—and has the interview of her life in two days. You

____ **a.** Tell her it doesn't matter; she'll get the job because she's an intelligent, creative, strong woman

____ **b.** Sympathize and suggest she call her dermatologist instead

____ **c.** Ask her to describe it exactly, then tell her which zit-zapping cream will clear it in two days, and how often to apply it

**9** How many bottles are in your shower?

____ **a.** Five or more—there's simply no such thing as enough shower gel.

____ **b.** Three to five—the basics plus a couple extra, for variety's sake.

____ **c.** Two to three—just the basics.

# Scoring

Give yourself the numerical value that matches each of your answers. Then add all nine scores together and use your total score to find your result category.

1. a – 3  b – 2  c – 1
2. a – 1  b – 2  c – 3
3. a – 2  b – 1  c – 3
4. a – 1  b – 3  c – 2
5. a – 3  b – 2  c – 1
6. a – 1  b – 2  c – 3
7. a – 2  b – 1  c – 3
8. a – 1  b – 2  c – 3
9. a – 3  b – 2  c – 1

(22–27 points)
## You Are Queen of the Product Junkies

Lip gloss, hair gel, eyeliner, wrinkle cream, moisturizer, self-tanner—you love it all. You get a rush from being the first to wear the lip color of the season, and you cherish the bottles that line your shower stall. You see, you sample, you buy, you glow; you start all over again. You're putting the girls at the Clinique counter through law school—and you're proud of it! Friends may murmur that your product mania indicates an unrealistic desire for perfection. Unrealistic? Pshaw! You know the power of perfectly applied highlighter, the necessity of having blotting papers within reach, and the allure of a dab of gloss placed just so. Let the naysayers walk around with frizzy hair and barefaced blemishes to make a pointless point—beauty is your art and beauty products are your muse. You know that you're not for a second bending to someone else's standard of beauty—you are using all the tools at your disposal to constantly evolve and recreate your own.

(15–21 points)
## You're a Product Aficionado

There's no doubt about it: You're no stranger to the thrill of unwrapping a new trendy lipstick. But you'll test and compare before you buy, then use that tube until it's gone (and can throw away the dregs without separation anxiety). For a quick change you'll mix that lipstick with a gloss you already have, instead of buying three more new lipsticks in similar shades. In short, products don't rule your universe. Sure, you have your product fantasies, but you temper them with a healthy dose of wallet reality. When the salesgirl at your favorite beauty counter asks for your name and address, you give it to her so you will receive mailings about new product releases or invitations to special in-store events. This keeps you in the "know" and alerts you to all-important "gift with purchase" (GWP) time! And you ask for samples every time you browse the counters.

**(9–14 points)**

## You're Addicted to . . . Simplicity

Products don't rule your world. You know which ones work for you, and you stick with them. But remember that some products can become less effective after repeated use. So if your favorite product isn't rocking your world lately, try shaking up your routine.

Your chic, simple style is admirable. It keeps you in classic form and prevents you from becoming a trend victim. That said, keep your look up-to-date; don't be afraid to test a new color palette once in a while. And if you're nervous about wasting your money, keep your eye out for freebies so that you can try before you buy. Or sit down for a makeover at your favorite cosmetics counter. It's fun! (GWP is a good acronym to know: gift with purchase!)

# What Lipstick Color Are You?

For many women, buying lipstick is somewhat of a science—you think about your skin tone, your clothing, your budget. But what about your personal style? Use this quiz to find the perfect color for your pucker, based on your personality.

**1** What's your "signature" shoe?

____ **a.** Stiletto

____ **b.** Mules

____ **c.** Chunky platform

____ **d.** Running shoe

____ **e.** Strappy sandal

**2** You're at a party and the hostess offers you an array of drink options. You choose

____ **a.** Cosmopolitan

____ **b.** Wine

____ **c.** Herbal energy drink

____ **d.** Juice

____ **e.** Soda

**3** What's your idea of a perfect afternoon?

____ **a.** Shopping, shopping, shopping

____ **b.** A picnic in the park

____ **c.** Checking out new art gallery exhibits

____ **d.** Scouring local flea markets for one-of-a-kind finds

____ **e.** Inline skating

**4** While shopping in a department store, you find the absolute perfect pair of pants, but sadly, they are way out of your budget. What do you do?

____ **a.** Push the limit on your charge card—they're worth it.

____ **b.** Go home and revamp a pair of old pants into the same style.

____ **c.** Feel better about taking a pass when you see two other girls trying on the same model—who wants what everyone else will be wearing?

____ **d.** Put them back on the rack—no pair of pants is worth going into debt.

____ **e.** Go out and find a great knockoff version at a lower price.

**5** You've got some time to kill at the nail salon. Which magazine do you flip through?

____ **a.** *Harper's Bazaar*

____ **b.** *Martha Stewart Living*

____ **c.** *Nylon*

____ **d.** *Real Simple*

____ **e.** *Cosmopolitan*

**6** It's your big debut at the karaoke bar. You belt out a song by

____ **a.** Madonna

____ **b.** Billie Holiday

____ **c.** Gwen Stefani

____ **d.** Jewel

____ **e.** Britney Spears

**7** Which movie title best describes your look?

____ **a.** *Some Like It Hot*

____ **b.** *Pretty in Pink*

____ **c.** *Wild at Heart*

____ **d.** *The Natural*

____ **e.** *Crazy/Beautiful*

**8** Which of these careers most appeals to you?

____ **a.** Clothing designer

____ **b.** Wedding planner

____ **c.** Activist

____ **d.** Adventure tour guide

____ **e.** Gossip columnist

**9** You're having a bad hair day. You

____ **a.** Call in sick

____ **b.** Wrap your hair in a Pucci scarf, à la Marilyn Monroe

____ **c.** Add some texturizing cream and work a messy "bedhead" look

____ **d.** Barely notice

____ **e.** Use some quirky, colorful barrettes to minimize the damage

**10** Which flavor of ice cream would most likely be in your freezer?

____ **a.** French vanilla

____ **b.** Coffee

____ **c.** Green tea

____ **d.** Lemon sorbet

____ **e.** Chocolate chip

# Scoring

Add up the number of As, Bs, Cs, Ds, and Es you chose. Find the category in which you had the most responses to determine your lipstick color—and what that reveals about you. Also check the other colors that may be right for you based on your responses.

## (Mostly As)
## Red Alert

For a fashion-savvy sister like you, a deep red lipstick is the obvious choice. Not only will this sizzling scarlet look great with all your designer duds, but the sleek packaging will look *trés* chic in your new Gucci clutch.

*Application tip:* Because this color is fairly intense, apply the lipstick first, then follow with a lip liner for a more streamlined look.

## (Mostly Bs)
## Pretty in Pink

Although you're totally in touch with the trends, you're still an old-fashioned girl at heart. For a classic like you, a pinkish lipstick is the answer. The soft, sexy rose will leave you with a pucker that looks highly kissable.

*Application tip:* Skip the liner and use a lip brush to apply this soft color to your lips for a "just bitten" look.

## (Mostly Cs)
## Passionate Plum

You like to push boundaries in your life and with your style. You use your clothes and makeup to make a statement; you don't want to blend in. A purple-hued lipstick will satisfy your need to stand out from the crowd. Go for an intense plum—the perfect shade for a wild child like you.

*Application tip:* After applying with a lip brush, top off the color with a light layer of sparkly lip gloss for added shine and instant appeal.

## (Mostly Ds)
## Barely Berry

You believe natural beauty is best. Not one to hide behind a lot of makeup or coiffed hair, you choose to keep things simple. For a down-to-earth woman like you, a translucent berry lipstick is best. Look for a shade that mimics the color of your natural lip, only a little bolder.

*Application tip:* Make sure to keep your lips color-ready by applying a light coat of lip balm with vitamins and natural oils underneath your lipstick. This will keep your lips soft and help your color go on more smoothly (so that you won't need to overapply).

(Mostly Es)

## Sheer Shimmer

Cyndi Lauper must have been talking to you when she sang, "Girls just want to have fun!" Never one to take style too seriously, you love the glitzy glamour of pop icons such as Gwen Stefani and Janet Jackson. That's why a clear lip lacquer loaded with sparkle is the perfect pick for you. Not only will it satisfy all of your glam-rock desires, it will give you an out-of-this-world smile.

*Application tip:* Keep the glitter on other areas of your face to a minimum. Too much sparkle can leave you looking like a shimmer-victim.

# What Fragrance Is Right for You?

The fragrance you wear should suit your personality and mood. Which scent is a perfect pick for you? Take this test to find out what to spritz on—and what to leave on the store shelves.

**1** **What type of music do you listen to most often?**

____ **a.** Dance music

____ **b.** R&B

____ **c.** Rock 'n' roll

____ **d.** Classical

____ **e.** World music

____ **f.** Latin/salsa

____ **g.** Jazz

**2** **Which of these foods would you prefer?**

____ **a.** A heaping bowl of fresh fruit—berries, plums, oranges, grapes, and apples

____ **b.** Comfort food like an all-American burger and fries or Grandma's meatloaf and mashed potatoes

____ **c.** Grilled salmon with vegetables

____ **d.** Continental classics like Chicken Cordon Bleu or rack of lamb

____ **e.** An artful array of sushi with steamed spinach or broccoli

____ **f.** Mexican, Indian, or Cajun dishes—the spicier the better!

____ **g.** Anything sweet, especially chocolate

**3** **What's your favorite drink?**

____ **a.** Beverages with a boost, such as an energy-enhancing fruit smoothie or a sports drink

____ **b.** A soothing cup of herbal tea

____ **c.** Bottled water

____ **d.** Champagne—for any occasion

____ **e.** A crisp glass of white wine

____ **f.** A dry red wine

____ **g.** Colas or coffee—the more caffeine the better

**4** **What's your favorite color?**

____ **a.** Orange

____ **b.** Green

____ **c.** Yellow

____ **d.** Pink

____ **e.** Blue

____ **f.** Red

____ **g.** Purple

**5** **What best describes your signature outfit?**

____ **a.** Warm-up suits, sweats, or anything made from polar fleece

____ **b.** Jeans and a T-shirt

____ **c.** Flirty skirts and beaded tops

____ **d.** Feminine floral sundresses

____ **e.** Luxurious basics such as silk knit dresses or casual cashmere slacks

____ **f.** All-black urban ensemble of leather or suede

____ **g.** Funky leopard-print jacket with a trendy velvet dress

**6** **What's your favorite workout?**

____ **a.** Intense sports, such as kickboxing or snowboarding

____ **b.** Golf or hiking

____ **c.** Aerobics classes

____ **d.** Power walking

____ **e.** Water sports, such as swimming and surfing

____ **f.** Balancing body work, such as yoga or Pilates

____ **g.** Dancing

**7** **What's your favorite type of weather?**

____ **a.** Bracing cold

____ **b.** Crisp fall weather when the leaves start to turn

____ **c.** Tropical, humid heat

____ **d.** Spring weather—not too hot, not too cold

____ **e.** Rainy, misty weather

____ **f.** Dry heat/Indian summers

____ **g.** Warm, pleasant, no-jacket weather

**8** **What's your favorite vacation spot?**

____ **a.** Mountains or adventure locations

____ **b.** Lakeside resort

____ **c.** Spa retreat

____ **d.** Countryside

____ **e.** Beach

____ **f.** Major international city or exotic location

____ **g.** Island getaway

**9** **When do you apply fragrance?**

____ **a.** After a workout

____ **b.** On weekends only

____ **c.** To jumpstart the day

____ **d.** All the time

____ **e.** Only at home

____ **f.** Before a date or a special occasion

____ **g.** At night

# Scoring

Add up the number of As, Bs, Cs, Ds, Es, Fs, and Gs you chose. Find the category in which you had the most responses to determine the right fragrance for you. Also check out the other scents that may work well for you, based on your responses.

### (Mostly As)
## Sporty Scents

Sporty scents fit your energetic and adventurous personality: choose ones composed of citrus fruits, light flowers such as lily of the valley or freesia, herbs, and green tea. Crisp, vibrant fragrances match your penchant for healthy food, vigorous workouts, and bright colors. You love the great outdoors, and even the wicked chills of winter won't keep you housebound.

*Sporty scents to try:* Tommy Hilfiger's Tommy Girl, Clinique Happy, Shiseido Energizing Fragrance.

### (Mostly Bs)
## Green Scents

Green, natural scents from the leaves and stems of plants combined with flowers like hyacinth or tea rose, reflect your down-to-earth attitude. Whether you're spending quality time with family or hiking around a lake in jeans and a T-shirt, light floral fragrances with a hint of woody richness perfectly suit your lifestyle. When the sun sets, simple pleasures abound, and you eagerly look forward to crisp fall evenings when you can wrap yourself in a wool blanket with a warm cup of tea and enjoy your favorite new CD.

*Green scents to try:* Chanel No. 19, Gucci Envy, Elizabeth Arden Green Tea.

### (Mostly Cs)
## Fruity Scents

Fruity scents, with notes of melon, raspberry, and apricots combined with flowers such as peony, rose, or magnolia, are the perfect complement to your bubbly personality. Nothing beats a high-energy aerobic workout to keep you looking fit and fabulous in flirty, feminine threads. You love all things tropical, which helps explain your fondness for steamy, summer heat. Clean, effervescent fragrances exude a sparkle similar to yours, and are the perfect complement for your energetic, healthy lifestyle.

*Fruity fragrances to try:* 2000 Fleurs by Creed, Spring Fever by Origins, Bobbi by Bobbi Brown Essentials.

## (Mostly Ds)
# Floral Scents

Floral scents, with notes of jasmine, orchid, violet, rose, sandalwood, musk, and vanilla, capture your loving, tender character. By day a country field filled with flowers appeals to your inner nature lover. When the sun sets, a candlelit dinner for two at the latest four-star restaurant is your idea of heaven. You let your inner beauty shine through by wearing delicate pinks and floral sundresses, and complement your look with fragrances that are as feminine and romantic as you are.

*Floral fragrances to try:* Eternity Rose Blush by Calvin Klein, Paris by Yves Saint Laurent, Beautiful by Estée Lauder.

## (Mostly Es)
# Marine Scents

Oceanic scents, combining notes of rain, ozone, melon, grapes, or cucumber with cyclamen, water lily, or honeysuckle, reflect your temperamental, artistic nature. Your multifaceted personality is reflected in your love of luxurious fabrics (think silk and cashmere), crisp colors such as blue and white, and exotic food. Your ideal scent is as multifaceted—and distinctive—as your personality.

*Marine scents to try:* Relaxing by Shiseido, Aqua di Gio by Georgio Armani, Cool Water Woman by Davidoff.

## (Mostly Fs)
# Woodsy Scents

Woodsy, warm scents, with rich notes of sandalwood, cedar, vetiver, patchouli, spicy cinnamon, clove or pepper, and vanilla, work well with your sensuous and loving personality. Spicy foods and red wine help ignite your warm character and reflect the rich nature of fragrances that suit your sophisticated lifestyle.

*Woodsy scents to try:* Sandalwood by Caswell Massey, Shalimar by Guerlain, Rapture by Victoria's Secret.

## (Mostly Gs)
# Sweet Scents

Sweet and yummy scents, composed of chocolate, caramel, honey, or vanilla, mirror your sexy and seductive moods. The sensuous beat of jazz music sets your heart racing as you dance the night away, while the lush feel of velvet and faux fur mirrors your yen for all things soft and decadent. Your signature scent reflects your favorite things in life—a little bit naughty, a little bit nice, and totally delicious.

*Sweet scents to try:* Lolita Lempicka, Baby Doll by Yves Saint Laurent, Angel by Thierry Mugler.

# Do You Need a Makeover?

When was the last time you updated your beauty routine or tried a new look? Trying new things and being on the lookout for new ideas is part of what keeps your look—and your attitude—vibrant. Do you need to stretch beyond your normal limits? Answer these questions to find out if you need a makeover—and if you're really ready for one.

**1** Your favorite lip color could be renamed

____ **a.** Rock 'n' roll

____ **b.** Oats 'n' honey

____ **c.** Sugar 'n' spice

**2** Your best friend is considering getting her navel pierced. Your first thought is

____ **a.** Copycat!

____ **b.** How much does that cost, anyway?

____ **c.** What a horrible place to get an infection!

**3** The last time you tried a new eye shadow was

____ **a.** When George Sr. was president

____ **b.** Just the other day—you and the department store makeup gal are so chummy, she even invited you to her bridal shower

____ **c.** Last season—you often see something in *Vogue* or *Allure* that you want to try

**4** The last time you went skinny-dipping you were

____ **a.** Five years old in your little back-yard pool from Kmart

____ **b.** Tipsy at a bonfire on the beach with your honey and your closest friends

____ **c.** At that after-party with those guys from that band

**5** **Your current hair color is**

____ **a.** A work of art

____ **b.** What you were born with or grew into

____ **c.** Within a few shades of your natural color (or what your natural color used to be!)

**6** **You entered a makeover contest and won a free tattoo. You**

____ **a.** Know just the kind you want—and where you want it

____ **b.** Are pretty sure they mean one of those temporary tattoos, right?

____ **c.** Pass on your prize—you weren't really into the makeover idea anyway

**7** **Your favorite nail polish at the salon is**

____ **a.** "Ballet Slippers"

____ **b.** "Wicked"

____ **c.** A French manicure

**8** **Your best friend is getting hair extensions and will pay for yours if you'll try them with her. You**

____ **a.** Are game, as long as they match your hair and are easy to take out

____ **b.** Are definitely there—all the celebrities wear them to movie premieres and you've been dying to try them

____ **c.** Would be happy to . . . go watch *her* get them while *you* get a manicure

**9** **The movie title that best describes your sex life is**

____ **a.** *Sense and Sensibility*

____ **b.** *America's Sweethearts*

____ **c.** *Bring It On*

**10** **You have a gift certificate for a salon treatment. You get**

____ **a.** A Brazilian bikini wax

____ **b.** A deep-tissue massage

____ **c.** A manicure/pedicure

## Scoring

Give yourself the numerical value that matches each of your answers. Then add all 10 scores together and use your total score to find your result category.

1. a – 3   b – 1   c – 2
2. a – 3   b – 2   c – 1
3. a – 1   b – 3   c – 2
4. a – 1   b – 2   c – 3

5. a – 3   b – 1   c – 2
6. a – 3   b – 2   c – 1
7. a – 1   b – 3   c – 2
8. a – 2   b – 3   c – 1
9. a – 1   b – 2   c – 3
10. a – 3   b – 2   c – 1

(24–30 points)

## Quick-Change Artist

You always keep your beauty repertoire up-to-date and are never afraid to risk something new—as long as it's part of your never-ending search for looks that rock! Your concern is not about trying a new you, it's about *which* new you to reveal. Because you're always all about trying the hottest trends, why not give your look—and your attitude—a style break and create a more relaxed you? You just might enjoy the carefree air that comes with wearing classic, natural colors and styles, and the free time that comes with a less experimental, more streamlined beauty regimen.

(17–23 points)

## Looking for a Little Something

Getting frequent manicures will keep your look polished, but that won't make your style current and fresh. It's time to throw your well-groomed self a curve and try something you normally wouldn't. Put yourself out on a beauty limb: Be less structured and more playful by revealing a sexier you. Or luxuriate in a more relaxed, natural you. You might be surprised by how much a little makeover can do for you—not to mention your love life and career. So give your beauty routine a twist and enjoy the extra appeal it gives you.

(10–16 points)

## In Need of Renovation

The thought of spicing up your look may be buried in your head somewhere, but you've always got an excuse—no time, no money, no ideas . . . no guts? You are perfectly primed to reveal a new you! What is your deepest, truest beauty wish? Whether you harbor a secret wish for a completely different hairstyle, a modern makeup look, or a downright sexier you, now's the time to go for it. You'll be amazed by what a makeover can do for your self-confidence, your love life, your career, and much more!

# 8

# Uncover Your Home Style

## And find out what your decor says about you

What's Your Decorating Personality?

Are You Addicted to Stuff?

Do You Have Good or Bad Feng Shui?

Is Your Bedroom a Love Nest or a Last Resort?

# What's Your Decorating Personality?

Is there any better way to learn more about a person than by looking at where she lives? What does *your* home say about you? Answer these questions and discover your decorating personality—and how to fill your home with furnishings that are true reflections of who you are.

**①** **Imagine that a friend is coming over for the first time. What part of the house *don't* you want her to see?**

____ **a.** Your bedroom—you can't even see the floor because there are clothes strewn everywhere.

____ **b.** Your drawers or cabinets—they're liable to be jam-packed with all the things you don't have room to display on your bookshelves.

____ **c.** Your kitchen—you just can't seem to get it to look and feel cozy.

____ **d.** The master bathroom—you don't want anyone to see the outdated fixtures until you get a chance to renovate.

____ **e.** Your kids' rooms—they're the only parts of the house that you can't control.

____ **f.** Your house is never "ready for prime time"—you'll just do a quick pick-up and hope for the best, or better yet, arrange to meet her out for coffee.

____ **g.** Your workspace—even though it's your favorite part of the house, you don't want anyone to see your various unfinished projects or your piles of supplies.

**②** **What's your favorite spot in your home?**

____ **a.** Your bathroom—your temple to yourself, filled with pretty things.

____ **b.** Your bookshelves—you love looking at them and getting to see all of the various things that are important to you on display.

____ **c.** Your living room—the place that most looks like the beautiful rooms you see in your favorite home catalogs and magazines.

____ **d.** The kitchen—you spend most of your time there.

____ **e.** Your closets—they're tidy and organized, and give you a sense of comfort and control.

_____ **f.** The couch—you love to flop there.

_____ **g.** Your workspace—the one place that's all your own and where you really get to express your creativity.

**3** **How would you describe your home's color palette?**

_____ **a.** Lots of different colors—whatever strikes your fancy

_____ **b.** Muted neutrals that show off your colorful collection of accessories and wall hangings

_____ **c.** Various hues of white

_____ **d.** Antique metallics

_____ **e.** Blacks and grays—sleek and clean

_____ **f.** You don't know much about color—you always leave your walls the same color as when you moved in

_____ **g.** Soft pastels

**4** **Which material does your home have the most of?**

_____ **a.** Animal skins (faux or real)

_____ **b.** Wood

_____ **c.** Metals

_____ **d.** Stone

_____ **e.** Glass

_____ **f.** Plastic

_____ **g.** Ceramics

**5** **Where do you do most of your home shopping?**

_____ **a.** You browse home stores until something jumps out at you.

_____ **b.** A different place every time—a garage sale, a catalog, or an interesting store you happen upon.

_____ **c.** The Pottery Barn or other mail order catalogs, but you're not afraid to mix in some pieces from Target or Ikea.

_____ **d.** Estate sales and auctions, although you have a lot of pieces that were handed down through your family.

_____ **e.** You're faithful to particular home lines—a designer or a particular store with its own unique aesthetic.

_____ **f.** You don't do a lot of home shopping—you make do with what you have.

_____ **g.** You love browsing arts and crafts fairs and picking through discount stores to see what treasures you can unearth.

**6** **What's your biggest obstacle to creating the home of your dreams?**

_____ **a.** By the time you create your "dream home," your tastes will have changed and you will be ready for a new theme.

_____ **b.** You like so many different types of things you don't know how you could ever make them all work together.

____ **c.** You want a stylish home, but you would never have the wherewithal to keep up with the latest home fashions.

____ **d.** You don't have the space for all the various rooms you long to have—formal living room, family room, dining room, and so on.

____ **e.** Your home could never live up to the ideal in your mind—you either can't afford it or don't know enough about design to make it happen.

____ **f.** You can't work up the energy to make it happen.

____ **g.** Your dream house is handcrafted, and you don't have the time to give it the personal attention it would need to be all that you want it to be.

**7** What types of items give you a sense of comfort and serenity?

____ **a.** Your fancy bath salts, aromatherapy candle, and fluffy bath pillow

____ **b.** A shrine of your own—an artfully displayed collection of treasured mementos

____ **c.** Candles everywhere

____ **d.** Throw blankets that match your decor

____ **e.** Gathered stones on a platter

____ **f.** Dimmer switches

____ **g.** Fresh flowers from the garden

**8** Where do you get decorating inspiration?

____ **a.** Sudden creative flashes—usually when shopping for home furnishings, but occasionally in the shower

____ **b.** From your various life experiences—perhaps a wall color inspired by the Tuscan sky, a chair picked up at the flea market, or shells collected from the beach

____ **c.** Magazines such as *Elle Décor,* TV shows such as *E! Celebrity Homes,* or even the Ikea catalog

____ **d.** Magazines such as *Architectural Digest* and *House Beautiful*

____ **e.** Browsing art galleries and cutting-edge, out-of-the-way stores

____ **f.** Nowhere—you wish that you had some decorating inspiration

____ **g.** Watching all the how-to shows on television—with a glue gun and a pair of scissors you can really make some great things

**9** Which celebrity's sense of style do you most admire?

____ **a.** Mary J. Blige

____ **b.** Cameron Diaz

____ **c.** Jennifer Aniston

____ **d.** Martha Stewart

____ **e.** Gwyneth Paltrow

____ **f.** Meg Ryan

____ **g.** Rosie O'Donnell

**⑩ It's time to buy a new couch. What is your plan of attack?**

____ **a.** You'll make it a point to stop by some home stores and see what jumps out at you—it won't take more than two trips.

____ **b.** You'll visit a lot of stores and sit on a lot of couches, then finally buy exactly what you want, even if you have to have it custom made (it's worth it for a couch that you'll love).

____ **c.** You'll browse through magazines for a style you like, then find the closest match at a department store.

____ **d.** You'll call an interior designer for professional advice.

____ **e.** You'll see what your favorite designers are doing this season, but you will have a hard time making a final decision—there are too many beautiful couches out there to decide quickly!

____ **f.** You'll go down to the nearest sleeper-sofa depot—you just don't want to spend a lot of money.

____ **g.** You'll consider a new slipcover or reupholstering before you commit to buying new.

# Scoring

Add up the number of As, Bs, Cs, Ds, Es, Fs, and Gs you chose. Find the category in which you had the most responses to determine your decorating personality. Also pay attention to the other categories in which you scored high, as they may reveal other reflections of who you are.

(Mostly As)
## Adventurer

Bold and eclectic, you probably love fashion. Your home may feel like your own personal movie set, with lots of dramatic pieces. You might be struck with an idea for the living room while you're in the shower or fall in love with an item that you spy in a store, leading to a whole new decorating theme. While you're strong on inspiration and a sense of your own taste, you're probably lacking in organization and follow-through. Try first to identify projects that are driving you crazy, then break them down into stages. Cleaning the closets and throwing old things away is always a good catalyst. One word of warning: Your strong sense of taste can lead you to be overly materialistic. You tend to buy things on a whim, which can also be bad for your budget. To get in touch with your spiritual side, try taking some of your precious possessions and making a small shrine. Declare a vanity shelf or tabletop your own. Gather small photos, beads, jewelry, perhaps a crystal. Spend some quiet time with your shrine to seek comfort and balance.

(Mostly Bs)
## Individualist

You don't fit into any one mold of decorative tastes—you're more concerned with finding just the right piece that really speaks to you rather than buying the whole matching set. With a carefully crafted collection of treasured items—mementos picked up on your travels or unique pieces that strike a sentimental chord—you are deliberate in your selections. The same way Cameron Diaz can combine vintage and Prada, you take elements from all over and use them to create a look that's all your own. You do need to be careful that you don't get too overwhelmed with things. A good way to keep your knick-knacks from taking over your home is to choose your favorites and put the rest in storage for a while. You can rotate them seasonally (pulling the quilts out in the fall, vintage planters in the spring) or whenever you need to mix things up. Give away any item that doesn't touch your soul in some way.

(Mostly Cs)
## Style Maven

Pulled-together and picture perfect, you love the *InStyle* magazine and *E! Television* features that offer sneak peeks into celebrities' homes. You are design-oriented and have plenty of style. You love the clean and pristine, so may want to focus on setting a mood and creating more comfort in your home. Liven things up with lots of plants and don't be afraid to let your home look like people actually live there: Throw pillows on the floor and an artfully arranged stack of books next to the bed make perfection look cozy. Keep lots of candles on hand. You can make candle lighting a ritual, and include a brief meditation or recital of a daily poem or quote.

Staying on top of home fashions has the potential to eat up a lot of money, but it doesn't have to. Remember: Doing it yourself is better than not doing it. Mistakes will happen, but learning on the job is part of the process.

(Mostly Ds)

# Traditionalist

You probably have a sense of nostalgia for the more settled and predictable world your parents and grandparents grew up in, where men wore hats and women wore pearls. You have a strong sense of history, and your home reflects it, with items such as matching sideboards with majestic Oriental vases and pieces handed down through the generations. You probably have items in your home that represent longevity, such as a stone fireplace or granite countertops, and your home is made for entertaining friends with a warm, welcoming hearth. While you may want your home to conform to the ideal in your head, time and money constraints probably force you to settle for less. Write down what you want to accomplish. Create a scrapbook for clippings that inspire you. Share your ideas with like-minded friends or professionals who will give you honest feedback. And realize that making a beautiful home is first about making you and your family comfortable. Save a wall for stylishly arranged snapshots of time spent together, and try arranging beautiful yet soft throws in the family room. And remember, no house is a home that hasn't had some mishaps—that ice cream stain on the sofa can remind you of the life that goes on in your home.

(Mostly Es)

# Modernist

Sleek and sophisticated, you love having a home that anticipates your every need—from a kitchen with the latest appliances to the perfect lighting in every room. You have a very specific aesthetic, with clean, beautiful lines and not a lot of fuss. Yet you are reflective and enjoy sensual pleasures. You may want to explore using sumptuous fabrics and complimentary colors to add warmth to your otherwise cool environment. A great way to add some life to your home is with elegant cut flowers such as calla lilies or with simple, well-trimmed plants such as a bonsai or even wheatgrass planted in a pot (very Zen!). While you know precisely what effect you are going for, the many choices you have to make along the way can paralyze you. Get a clear picture of the ideal in your head, then identify your key constraints. Finding the balance between what you want and what you have to work with helps facilitate decision-making. Too many choices are better than none. When you find yourself in an absolute choice-overload funk, choose the most simple and practical.

(Mostly Fs)
## Anything Goes

It's not that you don't care about your home, it's just that you don't have the inspiration to envision the home of your dreams, much less the time or energy to make it happen. There's nothing wrong with being easy-breezy: Look at Meg Ryan or Sandra Bullock, who have gone a long way with their simple, this-is-who-I-am style. When it comes to projects around the house, you are well-intentioned, but you don't make much progress. You have to accept that money and time determine home priorities. Do a focus group with your family. Take some time to plan one larger project. Don't worry if it can't get done all at once—works in progress can often lead to greater satisfaction. An easy and affordable way to add life to your home is with plants. And for a simple project you can do yourself, try installing dimmer switches. You'll be amazed by how dimmers in every room can create a nice atmosphere.

(Mostly Gs)
## Artisan

You are a romantic who loves anything handmade. With lots of soft pastels in your palette, you get energy from the sun and the sea. You are on a constant fact-finding mission for home inspiration, from how-to television shows, the local paper, or home magazines. If someone shows the way, you can make the rest happen. For you, the making of a home is a journey. It's a creative process that's never quite finished. Think of your home as a canvas telling a story about you, your family, and your experiences. But never let your dreams get in the way of practicality: Your sanctuary still has to function. With that in mind, you may want to work on your organization skills, to help you keep your various projects and supplies in order. An everyday way to add a natural touch to your home is fresh flowers. Nothing compares to flowers grown from plantings that were nurtured with your own hands.

# Are You Addicted to Stuff?

Before you go on your next shopping spree, take this test to find out if clutter is controlling your life—and learn how to get back on track.

**1** You love to read, and there are stacks of books on your night table.

____ **a.** Not true at all

____ **b.** A little bit true

____ **c.** Mostly true

____ **d.** You to a tee

**2** Your closet is filled to the rafters with clothing and shoes. You have clothes in all sorts of sizes in there.

____ **a.** Not true at all

____ **b.** A little bit true

____ **c.** Mostly true

____ **d.** You to a tee

**3** You haven't been able to pull your car into the garage in years—it's just such a great storage area.

____ **a.** Not true at all

____ **b.** A little bit true

____ **c.** Mostly true

____ **d.** You to a tee

**4** Your dining room table has become your office/file-storage area. You clear it off for major holidays.

____ **a.** Not true at all

____ **b.** A little bit true

____ **c.** Mostly true

____ **d.** You to a tee

**5** When you can't find a bill or a catalog, you sort through the piles on the kitchen counter.

____ **a.** Not true at all

____ **b.** A little bit true

____ **c.** Mostly true

____ **d.** You to a tee

**6** You love makeup. In fact, you still have the lipsticks you used a decade ago.

____ **a.** Not true at all

____ **b.** A little bit true

____ **c.** Mostly true

____ **d.** You to a tee

**7** Your sheets are threadbare, your towels have holes, and you can't fit another item into your linen closet.

____ **a.** Not true at all
____ **b.** A little bit true
____ **c.** Mostly true
____ **d.** You to a tee

**8** You've been meaning to check with your accountant about which receipts you need to keep. Yours date back to the first year you filed taxes.

____ **a.** Not true at all
____ **b.** A little bit true
____ **c.** Mostly true
____ **d.** You to a tee

**9** When you travel, you can never seem to get away with less than four bags.

____ **a.** Not true at all
____ **b.** A little bit true
____ **c.** Mostly true
____ **d.** You to a tee

**10** You still have your supplies from that class you took a few years ago, even though you're almost 100 percent sure you won't use them ever again.

____ **a.** Not true at all
____ **b.** A little bit true
____ **c.** Mostly true
____ **d.** You to a tee

**11** You tend to collect things, and your home looks messier than you'd like. Sometimes you feel a little depressed or overwhelmed when you look at the clutter that's piling up.

____ **a.** Not true at all
____ **b.** A little bit true
____ **c.** Mostly true
____ **d.** You to a tee

**12** Your magazine subscriptions save you a lot of money off the newsstand price. Unfortunately, there are stacks of magazines all over your living room.

____ **a.** Not true at all
____ **b.** A little bit true
____ **c.** Mostly true
____ **d.** You to a tee

# Scoring

Give yourself the numerical value that matches each of your answers. Then add all 12 scores together and use your total score to find your result category.

1. **a – 4 b – 3 c – 2 d – 1**
2. **a – 4 b – 3 c – 2 d – 1**
3. **a – 4 b – 3 c – 2 d – 1**
4. **a – 4 b – 3 c – 2 d – 1**
5. **a – 4 b – 3 c – 2 d – 1**
6. **a – 4 b – 3 c – 2 d – 1**
7. **a – 4 b – 3 c – 2 d – 1**
8. **a – 4 b – 3 c – 2 d – 1**
9. **a – 4 b – 3 c – 2 d – 1**
10. **a – 4 b – 3 c – 2 d – 1**
11. **a – 4 b – 3 c – 2 d – 1**
12. **a – 4 b – 3 c – 2 d – 1**

(39–48 points)

## In Control

You have obviously learned how to part with things that you simply don't need. Be careful to remember that not many people can say this. Which means that the people you love—and perhaps live with—are probably not as organized as you are. If your mate is mad about his old baseball cards or your best friend can't bear to part with her ratty sweaters from years ago, be patient. Convincing others of the thrill of de-cluttering takes time. Keep in mind that the best way to teach is by example—people who are drowning in a sea of stuff won't appreciate lectures. Addiction to stuff is a real addiction! And changing that requires a gentle touch.

(30–38 points)

## About Average

While your life isn't ruled by your possessions, you could use an organizing tune-up. Realize that it takes 21 consecutive days of repeating an action to make it a habit. Make a list of positive habits you'd like to develop and tackle one at a time. A few good organizational habits that make life easier include putting your keys in the same place every time you get home, taking out the garbage every day, never leaving dirty dishes in the sink, and never leaving clean oncs on the drain board. Master these simple tasks, and the energy in your home—and in your life—will make a major shift for the better.

(21–29 points)

## Living Dangerously

The amount of stuff you have is probably taking its toll on your general well-being. There's no need to panic—

getting control of your possessions is a great opportunity for emotional healing. Schedule the time to do some major clearing out. Here's a simple trick that may help jump-start the process: Make a list of all the areas of your home that need organizing, then prioritize that list. Are you frightened to confront the area most in need of organization? If the answer is yes, then start with the easiest task, and build your confidence until you're ready to tackle that most difficult one.

## (12–20 points)
### Addicted to Stuff

Your stuff is in danger of controlling your life. Freeing yourself from objects you have outgrown or no longer need will be a healing experience, as you let go of the past and move into the present. Answering these questions will shed light on how and why you created the situation you're living in now: What was your family home like when you were growing up? Was your mother a wonderful housekeeper? Have you ever been organized? If you used to be organized and aren't now, what changed? Do you have a physical or emotional issue that needs to be dealt with that may be controlling you now? If you are feeling overwhelmed, don't worry. Changing your ways will happen one small step at a time—you don't have to conquer the clutter in every area of your home immediately! But take that first small step to get you on your way to breaking free of your addiction to stuff—one item at a time.

# Do You Have Good or Bad Feng Shui?

Chances are you've heard of *feng shui*—the Chinese discipline that can teach you how to attract and enhance your life energy (called *chi*) according to how your home is arranged. Do you attract the chi you need for a healthy and happy life? Take this test and find out.

**1** **The TV in your house is**

____ **a.** In your bedroom, discreetly hidden

____ **b.** Tucked into a corner in the living/family room

____ **c.** In your bedroom in full view

____ **d.** The focal point in the living/family room

**2** **Which statement most closely reflects the art on your walls?**

____ **a.** There isn't much of it, but what is there you love.

____ **b.** It's left over from the last tenant or just something you stuck up haphazardly.

____ **c.** It is a true reflection of who or what you want to be in life, and the things and people that are important to you.

____ **d.** It symbolizes things you no longer want to associate yourself with (such as being single, because you're looking for love).

**3** **The plants in your house are**

____ **a.** Plentiful and doing pretty well

____ **b.** Mostly placed in one room or area of the house

____ **c.** Meager—you have only one or two that you've managed to keep alive

____ **d.** Nonexistent

**4** **The chair you sit in for work**

____ **a.** Has arms and a back, but wobbles

____ **b.** Has no arms and wobbles

____ **c.** Has no arms but is sturdy

____ **d.** Has arms and a sturdy back and doesn't wobble

**5** **In your office or cubicle**

____ **a.** Your back is to the door when you are sitting at your desk

____ **b.** Your desk is in line with the door or hall as if you're a pin at the end of a bowling lane

____ **c.** The door is to your side when you're at your desk

____ **d.** You can see the door as you sit at your desk but you are not in line with it

**6** **Your bed**

____ **a.** Has no headboard and is up against a solid wall

____ **b.** Has a sturdy headboard and is up against a solid wall

____ **c.** Has a headboard with a window above it

____ **d.** Has no headboard with a window above it

**7** **Your front door**

____ **a.** Never gets used

____ **b.** Is dusty and a little squeaky, but people use it

____ **c.** Is difficult to see from the outside because of all the plants and other objects in front of it, but people still use it

____ **d.** Is uncluttered, inviting from the street, and people use it

**8** **Your stove**

____ **a.** Has four or more working burners and a clean oven

____ **b.** Has four working burners and a pretty clean oven

____ **c.** Has four working burners and a somewhat messy oven

____ **d.** Has at least one broken burner and a greasy oven

**9** **When you're cooking at the stove, your view of the kitchen door is**

____ **a.** Partial

____ **b.** Almost full

____ **c.** Full

____ **d.** Nonexistent (you cannot see the door)

**10** **The closest description of your bedroom would be**

____ **a.** An extension of your closet—filled to the brim with stuff

____ **b.** Your favorite and most nurturing place in the world

____ **c.** The place where you do more work and working out than sleeping

____ **d.** A very efficient place to get ready for the day

**⑪ Your bathroom can best be described as**

\_\_\_\_ **a.** Neat and organized

\_\_\_\_ **b.** Bright and cheery

\_\_\_\_ **c.** Dark and moldy

\_\_\_\_ **d.** Dusty and filled with clutter

# Scoring

Give yourself the numerical value that matches each of your answers. Then add all 11 scores together and use your total score to find your result category.

1. a – 2   b – 4   c – 1   d – 3
2. a – 3   b – 2   c – 4   d – 1
3. a – 4   b – 3   c – 2   d – 1
4. a – 2   b – 1   c – 3   d – 4
5. a – 1   b – 2   c – 3   d – 4
6. a – 3   b – 4   c – 2   d – 1
7. a – 1   b – 3   c – 2   d – 4
8. a – 4   b – 3   c – 2   d – 1
9. a – 2   b – 3   c – 4   d – 1
10. a – 1   b – 4   c – 2   d – 3
11. a – 3   b – 4   c – 1   d – 2

(36–44 points)

## Fabulous Feng Shui

You are on the right feng shui track, and should be seeing the benefits. You probably have a satisfying job and are respected by those around you. Maintaining a clean, dust-free, and unobstructed front door is a good way to stay on the right career track. Your love life is probably not so bad either, as you manage to keep most non-love-related items *out* of the bedroom (workout equipment, work-related items, laundry). And while your friends may think you're crazy to dust your plants, the healthy greenery in your home is just another reason for the positive energy in your life. Stay diligent about keeping the clutter away, using your rooms for what they are designed for, and keeping your home light and cheery.

(27–35 points)

## Satisfactory Shui

Life is pretty good, but why stop there? Maximize your energy reserves by creating a consistent power position in life (face the door in *all* positions—while you cook, work, or sit up in bed) and you will see even better days. Keep up the clutter clearing and make every room in your home a place that you feel good about. You can boost your feng shui by adding some of the elements (fire, water, earth) in specific areas of your home. For instance, add a water feature (such as a picture of snow or a tabletop fountain) to the front center area of your home to improve your career. Or add fire (some candles, an image of fire, or the color red) to the back center of your home to enhance the way people see you.

## (19–26 points)
## Insufficient Shui

Sluggish is the word for your chi. No doubt your life feels unexceptional and unexciting: Your home decor could be to blame. If you have rooms that have incongruent uses (using your dining room as an office or your bedroom as a workout space), create separate spaces for each function, using screens and plants to divide the room if necessary. Or clear clutter elsewhere (try the attic or basement) to create additional space. Pay attention to cleaning, as dust and dirt slow down chi. Position your bed with your head next to a solid wall (headboard preferred) and place your chair at work so you can see the door but are not in line with it. And give your oven a good cleaning and make sure the burners (a symbol of wealth in the feng shui world) are intact. To improve feng shui, make sure that *everything* in your home (including garage and attic) is either necessary, has been used in the past year, or is beloved by you.

## (11–18 points)
## Poor Feng Shui

Your home and office decor is definitely not helping you lead a positive and satisfying life. People may not respect you as you think they should, or you get overlooked in your relationships or career. But simple things such as placing a mirror so you can see the door as you work will put you in a more powerful position. Getting a new desk chair that isn't falling apart and allows you to sit up straight will also improve your chi and your chances of career success. In the feng shui world, your surroundings, including your furniture, represent you—including how others see you, who you are, and what you think about yourself. Address the clutter in and around your home, and clear some out to allow opportunities to enter your life. Broken, out-of-date stuff is like a logjam in the river of chi. To add romance, remove pictures of ex-boyfriends and single women from the bedroom. If you're in search of a mate or want to feel closer to your significant other, decorate with items in sets of two, such as picture frames, lamps, or candles. Light is another traditional cure that can rev up chi, so consider higher-wattage lights. A small nightlight can go a long way, too.

# Is Your Bedroom a Love Nest or a Last Resort?

The aura and style of your bedroom can predict a lot about the success (or lack thereof) of your love life—present and future. Does your boudoir invite intimacy—or an exterminator? Answer these questions to find out if your sleeping quarters are sabotaging your love life.

**1** Your bedroom television is

____ **a.** At the foot of your bed

____ **b.** Nonexistent—you keep the TV in the living room

____ **c.** Tucked in a corner

**2** The last time you bought flowers for your bedroom

____ **a.** You hadn't thrown out your last bouquet yet.

____ **b.** You thought, "I have to do this more than once every few weeks."

____ **c.** You've never bought flowers for your bedroom, ever.

**3** What's the pillow situation on your bed?

____ **a.** You have two or three, but one's a little flat.

____ **b.** You have one much-loved pillow dating from the days when you slept with a teddy bear.

____ **c.** You have a mountain of fluffy, sleep-worthy cushions.

**4** The windows in your bedroom are treated with

____ **a.** Unadorned mini-blinds, perfect for keeping the light out

____ **b.** Curtains in a fabric you love, perfect for creating a cozy, dim atmosphere

____ **c.** Opulent, thick drapes, perfect for keeping things dark and mysterious

**5** Your bed is

____ **a.** Fit for an empress

____ **b.** A twin size

____ **c.** Comfy but nothing special

**6** Your mattress is

____ **a.** On the floor

____ **b.** A double, with just the firmness you like

____ **c.** King-sized or full of water

**7** Your sheets are

____ **a.** Satin, silk, or Egyptian cotton—nothing but the best for you

____ **b.** Smooth, fresh, and delicious to slide into

____ **c.** The ones you took to college and/or decorated by hand

**8** If you want some music in your bedroom

____ **a.** You turn up the stereo in the living room and keep the door open

____ **b.** You grab the remote for your state-of-the-art, discreetly hidden sound system with 25-CD changer

____ **c.** You turn on the bedside radio

**9** What creates your bedroom's signature scent?

____ **a.** The perfume you spray on in the morning

____ **b.** Your laundry hamper

____ **c.** The candles you love to light at night

**10** If you were preparing your bedroom for a special night with your sweetheart, your first step would be

____ **a.** Scattering rose petals on the bed

____ **b.** Lighting a candle or turning on a soft-glowing lamp

____ **c.** Shoving some stuff into the closet

## Scoring

Give yourself the numerical value that matches each of your answers. Then add all 10 scores together and use your total score to find your result category.

1. a – 1   b – 3   c – 2
2. a – 3   b – 2   c – 1
3. a – 2   b – 1   c – 3
4. a – 1   b – 2   c – 3
5. a – 3   b – 1   c – 2
6. a – 1   b – 2   c – 3
7. a – 3   b – 2   c – 1
8. a – 1   b – 3   c – 2
9. a – 2   b – 1   c – 3
10. a – 3   b – 2   c – 1

## (24–30 points)
## Borderline Bordello

Diva, you certainly know how to set a stage! You love to create a mood, and you thrive on sensual surprises. But while your passion for passionate milieu is admirable, your man may not be prepared for the elaborateness of your lair. You don't want to scare him away or cause him performance anxiety! Tone it down a notch and watch the bedroom behavior turn from self-conscious to sensational.

## (17–23 points)
## Flirty Funhouse

You know that the best love nest is subtle, inviting, and hard to resist: The little touches go a long way. While you're not interested in transforming your bedroom into a sex siren's lair, you do like to add special touches when the mood and the man are right. Be sure to nurture *yourself* with a few of those relaxing and mood-setting treats once in a while, if you're not doing so already. Your bedroom should be a sanctuary for you—as well as for anyone who shares your sheets.

## (10–16 points)
## Desire Disaster Zone

There's a saying that goes, "Better to light a candle than to curse the darkness." In your case, you may be better off in the dark so that you can hide your unsexy surroundings. But don't despair. Setting the mood for romance can go a long way toward inciting it. Try recreating your love nest from the bottom up: clear the clutter, put the laundry in the bathroom, and invest in some sensuous sheets. Love and passion will surely follow!

# 9

# Make Your Wedding Dreams Come True

**And be a fabulous bride (or bridesmaid)!**

What's Your Wedding Style?

Are You Bridesmaid Material?

The Bridezilla Test: Is She a Bad Bride?

Bridal Beauty: What's Your Style?

# What's Your Wedding Style?

Before you can plan your big day, you need to know what type of wedding is right for you. Determining the overall style will help you make all of the other important planning decisions, such as choosing a dress, hiring a caterer, picking the flowers, and so on. Take this test to discover your wedding style and get ready to plan your big day!

**1** **Your dream dress will make you look**

____ **a.** Casual yet incredibly elegant

____ **b.** Like a princess

____ **c.** Sleek and sophisticated

**2** **Your bridal party wish list includes**

____ **a.** As many girlfriends as you can fit at the altar

____ **b.** No one—you're not having a wedding party at all

____ **c.** Just your sister or best friend

**3** **Do you want your groom to see you before you walk down the aisle?**

____ **a.** Absolutely—after all, it's not like it's any big secret who he's marrying.

____ **b.** Sure, but only if you can find a way to make that first-glimpse moment special.

____ **c.** No way! It's bad luck.

**4** **Your perfect bridal shower would be**

____ **a.** A fun evening of cocktails and hors d'oeuvres, with a coed guest list

____ **b.** A surprise gathering of girls, thrown by your maid of honor at your favorite restaurant

____ **c.** Nonexistent—you're not into the whole girls and gifts thing

**5** **For the first dance, you think the best way to be introduced is**

____ **a.** First dance? Forget it! You just want to get out on the dance floor and party.

____ **b.** By your first names—you may not change your last name anyway.

____ **c.** As Mr. and Mrs., of course. You can't wait to be announced as a married couple.

**6** One of your favorite weddings of all time was

____ **a.** The elegant at-home reception in *Father of the Bride,* starring Steve Martin (or Spencer Tracy in the earlier version)

____ **b.** Cindy Crawford and Rande Gerber's—how can you beat being barefoot on the beach when you say your vows?

____ **c.** Jennifer Aniston and Brad Pitt's—after all, she paired a floor-length white gown with suede high-heel sandals by shoe designer Manolo Blahnik!

**7** When it comes to Emily Post–type wedding etiquette, you

____ **a.** Think that what Emily says goes

____ **b.** Are comfortable revising "rules" that don't make sense for you

____ **c.** Don't plan to read—or follow—a word of such outdated protocol

**8** When you think of your reception, what comes to mind?

____ **a.** A reggae band and Jamaican food, or something equally different and festive

____ **b.** Music from swing to alternative rock to hip-hop, an eclectic buffet, and a dance with your mom as well as your dad

____ **c.** Six-piece band, sit-down dinner, cake-cutting moment—the works

**9** What types of gifts do you plan to register for?

____ **a.** Normal stuff like china, crystal, and pots and pans—that seems to be the way to go

____ **b.** Some kitchen and household items, plus some unique items—maybe exercise equipment, garden gear, or other hobby-related things

____ **c.** If you register at all, you may ask guests to contribute to your honeymoon fund, or to send checks to your favorite charity

**10** A destination wedding on a faraway isle sounds like

____ **a.** A great idea

____ **b.** An option, but only if your parents give you too much grief

____ **c.** A honeymoon, not a wedding

**11** Your dream guest list includes

____ **a.** 100 to 150 family members and friends

____ **b.** 25 to 50 guests, tops

____ **c.** Just about every name in your address book

**⑫ Who do you think should pay for your wedding?**

____ **a.** Just the two of you—after all, you're the ones getting married

____ **b.** Whoever wants to—any or all of your parents, the two of you, or a combination

____ **c.** Your parents—they've been waiting years to throw this bash

**⑬ You want the men at your wedding to look**

____ **a.** Neat and comfortable—you would be happy if they all wore nice dark suits

____ **b.** Classy and formal—you picture lots of tuxes, maybe the wedding party in tails

____ **c.** Hip and happy—if they want to show up in khakis, fine, as long as everyone has a good time

**⑭ The topper on your wedding cake will be**

____ **a.** Something fun that really reflects your personalities

____ **b.** Flowers, flowers, and more flowers

____ **c.** The traditional bride and groom

# Scoring

Give yourself the numerical value that matches each of your answers. Then add all 14 scores together and use your total score to find your result category.

1. **a – 2 b – 3 c – 1**
2. **a – 3 b – 1 c – 2**
3. **a – 1 b – 2 c – 3**
4. **a – 2 b – 3 c – 1**
5. **a – 1 b – 2 c – 3**
6. **a – 3 b – 1 c – 2**
7. **a – 3 b – 2 c – 1**
8. **a – 1 b – 2 c – 3**
9. **a – 3 b – 2 c – 1**
10. **a – 1 b – 2 c – 3**
11. **a – 2 b – 1 c – 3**
12. **a – 1 b – 2 c – 3**
13. **a – 2 b – 3 c – 1**
14. **a – 1 b – 2 c – 3**

(33–42 points)

## Cinderella Style

You've likely been dreaming of your wedding day since you were a little girl, when you and your friends threw napkins over your heads and pretended they were veils. So it shouldn't be any surprise to you—or anyone who knows you well—that you're a traditional wedding type. What would your wedding day be without a walk down the aisle to "Here Comes the Bride," the bouquet toss, a dance with Dad, and a grand cake-cutting moment? As long as your groom agrees with your traditional plan, you're all set. And going the traditional route often makes planning easier. But remember that your traditional wedding can include elements that truly reflect who you and your groom are and why you love each other. Consider serving your favorite food or adding a reflection of your ancestry to make your wedding extra special.

## (23–32 points)
### Tradition Meets Trendy

Your style is "tradition with a twist"— you're not ready to forgo tradition, but you feel strongly that your wedding should reflect your personality and your groom's, as well as your modern lifestyle and relationship. While you may not feel comfortable forcing all your single female friends to fill the dance floor and scramble to catch your bouquet, you might like the idea of sharing a first dance with your new husband. Nowadays it's completely acceptable for brides to revise traditions: You can include some of the common and familiar elements that work for you and still have the freedom to make changes.

After all, many brides these days have to figure out ways to involve parents, step-parents, and often their own children in their wedding day—something those dusty old etiquette tomes don't cover.

## (14–22 points)
### Modern-Day Diva

You're anything but traditional, so why should your wedding follow an old-fashioned formula? Good thing just about anything goes these days when it comes to weddings. You and your fiancé may want to scout out a unique wedding location or have a wedding with a crazy theme (a Halloween wedding with everyone in costume, or a surprise wedding where the guests don't even know they'll be witnessing your nuptials). Whatever you do, you want to make sure that your personalities come through loud and clear. It's important for you and your fiancé to get your ideas for your big day clearly mapped out and agreed on before you start bringing in service providers, and be sure those pros understand your vision. Let the true meaning of the day shine through—you don't want your guests to be so blown away by your funky, nontraditional ensemble that they forget what they're all gathered for.

# Are You Bridesmaid Material?

Always a guest, never a bridesmaid? Just appointed to be a member of the bride's inner circle and wondering if you can live up to the honor? Answer these questions and discover your bridesmaid potential—before you buy that poufy pink dress.

**1** You've had a really bad day. Just when you're about to go home and dive into a pint of chocolate-chocolate chip, a friend calls with a plea: "Can you please meet for coffee?" It's an emergency (a love-life crisis). What do you do?

____ **a.** Meet her, of course, and order yourself an extra-special coffee drink in lieu of ice cream.

____ **b.** Decline a meeting but muster whatever energy you can to spend time helping her over the phone.

____ **c.** Prescribe a quart of Cherry Garcia and tell her you're wiped and will talk to her tomorrow.

**2** You're planning a vacation with some girlfriends. One votes for a chic and costly beach spot; another wants to go low cost and casual; you could go either way. It's up to you to make the call. What do you do?

____ **a.** Draw straws—you want to be fair.

____ **b.** Choose your destination—hey, the planner gets the perks!

____ **c.** Find someplace middle-of-the-road and hope they'll both be happy.

**3** A small group of your friends have rented a vacation house and have invited you to join them. The price is steep and you can't really afford it. But they're putting the pressure on. What do you do?

____ **a.** Feel offended that your friends would ask you to do something you clearly can't afford—and let them know it.

____ **b.** Talk to the trip organizer and see if you can join them for only a few days—as many as you can comfortably afford.

____ **c.** Decline graciously—you'd love to go, but a vacation just doesn't fit into your budget.

**4** Your close friend just got a big promotion and it's all she talks about—day in, day out, week after week. It's as if there's nothing else in her life, and it's driving you crazy. Do you say something?

____ **a.** Not yet—she's excited and nervous. You'll give it a few more weeks before you nicely explain to her that hearing about her job 24/7 is beyond the call of duty.

____ **b.** Never—what are friends for, if not to listen and be supportive?

____ **c.** Definitely—you can't be a good friend under these circumstances (you're starting to really dislike her!).

**5** In your opinion, sororities are

____ **a.** A great way for young women to bond and create a pseudo family life at college

____ **b.** A good choice for some people, unnecessary for others

____ **c.** An obnoxious continuation of discriminatory high school cliques

**6** For the annual office party, your boss wants everyone in your department to dress alike—the company has been doing it that way for years. You will need a new outfit. What do you do?

____ **a.** Fake it; what you have in your closet will have to be close enough.

____ **b.** Skip it; you have no interest in accommodating such a ridiculous tradition.

____ **c.** Buy it; you can't say no to the boss.

**7** The biggest party you've ever been in charge of throwing involved

____ **a.** Making reservations for 10 friends at a nearby restaurant

____ **b.** Tossing chips and dip in bowls, ordering some pizza, and opening a few bottles of soda for friends

____ **c.** Doing a complete Martha: arranging several courses (either homemade or ordered), serving appropriate beverages, coordinating tableware, and so on

**8** If asked to choose the perfect profession for you, your friends would say you should be

___ **a.** An entrepreneur—you can turn just about anything into a winning proposition.

___ **b.** A therapist—you know how to listen, calm frazzled nerves, and otherwise fix crisis situations.

___ **c.** A temp—you could decide each morning whether or not you feel like working and never be at anyone else's beck and call.

**9** When you set out on a shopping spree to find the perfect outfit, dress, or shoes, you're prepared to

___ **a.** Spend hours looking until you find it—your energy is limitless when you're on a shopping mission

___ **b.** Check out a set number of stores and head home empty-handed if you haven't succeeded by then; there's always tomorrow

___ **c.** Spend hours looking, but after an hour or so with no luck, you're usually too tired and disappointed to continue

**10** The annual charity run is coming up. You participate by

___ **a.** Signing up to run when you're asked

___ **b.** Posting flyers, being among the first to sign up, and rallying your friends to follow suit

___ **c.** Making sure you have another engagement on the day of the run

## Scoring

Give yourself the numerical value that matches each of your answers. Then add all 10 scores together and use your total score to find your result category.

1. a – 3   b – 2   c – 1
2. a – 2   b – 1   c – 3
3. a – 1   b – 3   c – 2
4. a – 2   b – 3   c – 1
5. a – 3   b – 2   c – 1
6. a – 2   b – 1   c – 3
7. a – 1   b – 2   c – 3
8. a – 2   b – 3   c – 1
9. a – 3   b – 2   c – 1
10. a – 2   b – 3   c – 1

## (24–30 points)
## Bridesmaid from Heaven

You have all the qualities necessary to be a first-rate bridesmaid—you're patient, generous, sympathetic, and a hard worker. Good thing, because being a bridesmaid is not a walk in the park—or a simple stroll down the aisle. While a handful of brides require very little from their attendants, most come armed with a long to-do list for every bridesmaid. This is actually useful, as it's easier to fulfill your responsibilities when you know what they are. (If you're ever a bridesmaid and the bride doesn't specify what she expects of you, be sure to ask.) No matter what your to-do list includes—shopping for her wedding gown, planning a bachelorette party, or tracking down the perfect satin pump—you'll be crossing tasks off your list with ease and enthusiasm. Any bride would be lucky to have you in her wedding party!

## (17–23 points)
## Bridesmaid from the Real World

Even if you don't have a closet full of pastel bridesmaid gowns from past strolls down the aisle, that doesn't mean you wouldn't make a great attendant. You're tuned in to some of the most important rules of bridesmaid play, including fairness and friendly support. Plus you go the extra mile on occasion and give friends the benefit of the doubt whenever possible. However, your habit of being honest and upfront—about your opinions, a sticky situation, and so on—may cause a clash if the bride is looking for unconditional bridesmaid love (as in no judgments, no criticism, just pure, blind dedication). Still, any bride who's looking for a friend with a good head on her shoulders to see her through a pressure-filled time should look to you.

## (10–16 points)
## Bridesmaid from Hell

It doesn't look as if you're cut out to be a member of the bridal party. A lot of work is involved in being a bridesmaid. Typical duties include helping with a variety of tasks (from finding bridesmaids' gowns to reserving hair appointments for the bridal party on the wedding day), offering advice and emotional support, helping plan the bachelorette party and shower, and being there for the bride. The tricky part is that not all brides act like true-blue buddies during the engagement period.

With all that wedding pressure, some brides-to-be forget the rest of the world exists, or get so panicked they seem on the verge of a nervous breakdown. They all come out of it—at least in time for the honeymoon—but dealing with this takes a certain kind of person . . .

probably not you. So if a friend asks you to be in her wedding party, you might want to decline. Unless the bride has a wedding organizer planning her big day (and therefore doesn't need your help at all), you'll both be better off.

# The Bridezilla Test: Is She a Bad Bride?

Brides come in all shapes and sizes. But when it comes to attitude, most brides fall into one of three categories—good, bad, and worse. Find out if an upcoming wedding has transformed someone you know into a bride-gone-berserk!

**1** One of the bridesmaids shows up an hour late at the dress fitting for the gowns. The bride reacts by

____ **a.** Saying sarcastically, "Nice of you to show up."

____ **b.** Saying nonchalantly, "Glad you could make it."

____ **c.** Saying with relief, "Phew, you made it."

**2** At a restaurant, you peer over the top of your menu at the bride and ask, "What are you having for dinner?" The bride answers

____ **a.** "What do you think I'm having? A piece of lettuce is all I can eat these days if I want to fit into my gown!"

____ **b.** "Something light—I want to look my best for the pictures, especially in my snug dress."

____ **c.** "I was thinking about the hamburger and fries. What about you?"

**3** One of the bridesmaids informs the bride that she'll be eight months pregnant at the wedding. What does the bride do?

____ **a.** Congratulates her with no mention of the wedding

____ **b.** Asks her if she'll be comfortable walking down the aisle in that condition

____ **c.** Kicks her out of the wedding party

**4** When the bride is choosing dresses for her bridesmaids, she considers

____ **a.** Color, cut, and comfort—she wants her bridesmaids to look and feel good in what she chooses

____ **b.** Price—she's really only concerned that her bridesmaids not spend a mint

____ **c.** Color and style—she wants the dresses to match the colors and look of her wedding

**5** If you were to ask the bride about her biggest pre-wedding wish, it would be

____ **a.** That everyone would stop bothering her and just let her plan her day her way

____ **b.** That the wedding goes smoothly

____ **c.** That she gets the promotion at work she's been striving for

**6** When you ask the bride if she's stressed out about all her pre-wedding tasks, her response is:

____ **a.** "Yes, but I'm trying to relax so I can enjoy the good parts."

____ **b.** "No, should I be?"

____ **c.** "Duh! What do you think?"

**7** The band is charging a small fortune, the invited guests aren't replying, and the florist says he can't possibly get the exotic flowers the bride wants on her wedding day. You know all of this because

____ **a.** The bride mentioned she's upset about how things are developing

____ **b.** The bride has complained about each difficult development to practically every person she knows

____ **c.** The groom is really stressed out and called you to grumble (the bride hasn't uttered a word)

**8** As a shower gift, you *really* want to give the bride

____ **a.** Something off her registry

____ **b.** A massage to help her relax

____ **c.** Valium and a trip to the shrink

**9** Your friend the bride brings to mind

____ **a.** Elizabeth Taylor in *Father of the Bride*—she's pretty much your classic, likeable bride

____ **b.** Elsa Lanchester in *The Bride of Frankenstein*—she bears a scary resemblance to that hissing, shrieking costar

____ **c.** Julia Roberts in *My Best Friend's Wedding*—she's so relaxed about making decisions, it's almost like it's not her wedding

## Scoring

Give yourself the numerical value that matches each of your answers. Then add all nine scores together and use your total score to find your result category.

1. a – 3  b – 1  c – 2
2. a – 3  b – 2  c – 1
3. a – 1  b – 2  c – 3
4. a – 2  b – 1  c – 3
5. a – 3  b – 2  c – 1
6. a – 2  b – 1  c – 3
7. a – 2  b – 3  c – 1
8. a – 1  b – 2  c – 3
9. a – 2  b – 3  c – 1

(22–27 points)

## Bride from Hell

Your friend has a common case of bad-bride syndrome. Symptoms include a short temper, elevated stress level, and the unrealistic expectation that everyone on the planet wants to hear every last detail of her big day. By pouting, worrying, or arguing with others, bad brides can make wedding planning a nightmare for everyone involved. They can even ruin their own wedding day with these antics. What can you do about a bride-gone-bad? If you're not in the wedding party, you're in luck: Steer clear until post-honeymoon, when your friend will be back to her old self. If you're a maid or matron of honor, you're going to have to glue a smile on your face and forge ahead. Try not to take it personally or let it affect your friendship. Beneath all those layers of tulle and tension, your old friend is in there somewhere. Good luck!

(15–21 points)

## Average Engaged Gal

Your friend may have a bit of wedding-on-the-brain, but that's normal: Getting married is a big deal, and it's rarely free of at least a few narcissistic moments. Along with the logistics of planning the wedding (the biggest party she'll ever throw), she's also preparing to make a huge commitment. With all of that on one person's shoulders, you can almost understand why good brides go bad. But your friend seems to have her act under control: She may be somewhat obsessed and even overwhelmed, but she's trying her best not to drive everyone around her crazy. The best thing you can do now? Listen to her wedding stories and try to help, but encourage her to do non-wedding activities to take her mind off of her impending nuptials.

(9–14 points)

## Blasé Bride

Are you *sure* your friend is getting married? She's acting so unlike a bride-to-be, someone may want to remind her that she's got a wedding to plan in her not-too-distant future. While relaxed brides are certainly a pleasure to be around, those as cavalier and clueless as your friend seems to be are worrisome—and can make those pre-wedding months tricky for friends and family. Sometimes it's harder to know how to help someone when they won't give you any direction. (And you can't help wondering if she's excited about her betrothed and if she really should have said yes.) Then there's the question of the wedding. If she's got an elopement hidden up her sleeve, fine. But if she's supposed to be getting down to wedding planning business (and telling close friends and family what's expected of them), you may have to not-so-gently nudge her toward nuptial land.

# Bridal Beauty: What's Your Style?

Here comes the bride all dressed in . . . What, exactly, will you be wearing when you take that walk down the aisle? Answer these questions and discover your bridal style. It will make shopping for a gown and all those accessories so much easier. Plus, you'll find extra end-of-quiz perks for brides-to-be: makeup tips for the big day!

**1** **Which celebrity wedding made you green with envy?**

____ **a.** Drew Barrymore and Tom Green walking down the grassy aisle at sunset atop a Malibu cliff

____ **b.** Celine Dion and Rene Angelil in Vegas with a scene right out of *A Thousand and One Nights*—the Berber tents, the Arab-style chapel, the camels and exotic birds, not to mention the belly dancers . . . wow!

____ **c.** Princess Di and Prince Charles (yes, even with the unfairytale ending)— the dress, the horse-drawn coach, the old-world style

____ **d.** Madonna and Guy Ritchie going elegant at Skibo Castle in Dornoch, Scotland

**2** **When you were a little girl, you dreamed of becoming**

____ **a.** A veterinarian

____ **b.** A princess

____ **c.** An architect

____ **d.** A movie star

**3** **If the beauty police raided your bathroom shelves, which crime would you be charged with?**

____ **a.** A cover-up—you've got too much makeup, just what are you trying to hide anyway?

____ **b.** Lewd and lascivious behavior— with all those glitter gels and false lashes, you must be up to no good.

____ **c.** Negligence—your bare shelves are a beauty no-no.

____ **d.** Grand theft—no normal person could afford to *buy* that many bath and body treatments.

**4** **Which of these meals would you be most likely to order?**

____ **a.** Sushi

____ **b.** Filet mignon

____ **c.** Gourmet pizza

____ **d.** Veggie burger

**5** **If you could splurge on one major indulgence for your big day, what would it be?**

____ **a.** Your own hair and makeup team

____ **b.** Flowers, flowers, and more flowers

____ **c.** A sleek Vera Wang original

____ **d.** A string quartet to play you down the aisle

**6** **Which one of these colors would you never, ever, in a million years, pick for your bridesmaids' dresses?**

____ **a.** Pink

____ **b.** Lavender

____ **c.** Light blue

____ **d.** Black

**7** **A bride should wear her hair**

____ **a.** In a tasteful up 'do

____ **b.** Crimped and a little crazy

____ **c.** Loose and natural

____ **d.** Sleek and straight

**8** **What's your idea of the perfect honeymoon?**

____ **a.** Hiking in the Swiss Alps

____ **b.** Lounging on the beach in Brazil

____ **c.** Touring the Italian countryside

____ **d.** Shopping and fine dining in Paris

**9** **Forget about that tired cover band—which of these superstar performers would you choose to rock your reception?**

____ **a.** The pop stars of the moment

____ **b.** Your favorite country band

____ **c.** A mega-star (like Madonna) who's sure to impress your guests

____ **d.** A smooth crooner who can really sing the classics

# Scoring

Give yourself the numerical value that matches each of your answers. Then add all nine scores together and use your total score to find your result category.

1. a – 1  b – 2  c – 3  d – 4
2. a – 1  b – 3  c – 4  d – 2
3. a – 3  b – 2  c – 1  d – 4
4. a – 4  b – 3  c – 2  d – 1
5. a – 2  b – 1  c – 4  d – 3
6. a – 4  b – 3  c – 2  d – 1
7. a – 3  b – 2  c – 1  d – 4
8. a – 1  b – 2  c – 3  d – 4
9. a – 2  b – 1  c – 4  d – 3

## (30–36 points)
## The Chic City Chick

Maybe you never thought you were the marrying type, but now you find yourself getting ready to take that walk down the aisle. Never fear, wearing a white dress doesn't mean being smothered in ruffles and lace. For an urban girl like you, think simple and chic. A sexy silk shantung suit or sleek knee-length strapless dress are great alternatives. As long as you love the dress and it makes you feel special, that's all that matters. Go for the unexpected in shoes; a retro pointed-toe heel or a mod Mary Jane will help make a statement. Keep your makeup modern and minimal like the rest of your outfit. A light tinted moisturizer, a bit of bronzer, a sleek swipe of eyeliner, and a bold bright lip are all you need to look picture-perfect!

## (23–29 points)
## The Storybook Princess

An old-fashioned girl at heart, you want your special day to be steeped in elegance and tradition. You love the thought of transforming yourself into a timeless bride. You'll feel equally regal in a gown with a full tulle skirt or long, flowing train and a beaded corset top. And don't skip on any of the trimmings—go for the veil, tiara, and gloves. Sleek satin heels with a pointed toe are the perfect footwear for your stroll down the aisle. To complete your blushing bride look, keep your makeup soft and dewy. Use a light foundation and cream blush in a warm rose color that compliments your complexion, and keep your eyes soft and natural by using shadows in warm natural shades. Polish off your pucker with a sheer lipstick in a soft red.

(16–22 points)
## The Vegas Showgirl

You like your glamour and glitz, so why not turn your special day into an all-out extravaganza? Your dress should be anything but demure. Go for a sexy slip dress with a daring bare-it-all back or try a form-fitting strapless number in a satin that really shimmers. A veil is out of the question. Skip the headwear altogether and go for a crystal choker or maybe a few '20s-style jewel-encrusted bangles. Your shoes should be high and very sexy, but fairly comfy, because you'll probably be partying well into the night. Try a strappy sandal with rhinestone accents. Remember that although you like to sparkle, keep the glitter and shimmer to a minimum, because it can look too "reflective" in pictures. Create drama by lining your eyes with a liquid liner and sliding on high-shine lip gloss in pouty pink.

(9–15 points)
## The Flower Child

With the sky overhead and carpet of green grass, you'll be one with nature as you float down the aisle in a flowing gossamer gown. Nothing too fussy—a bared shoulder or a delicate cap sleeve will help transform your special day into a midsummer night's dream. And forget the froufrou veil—a wreath of fresh flowers will be the perfect accessory for your soft hairstyle. As for shoes, try a barely there sandal or maybe skip them all together and go barefoot—just don't forget to get an extra-special prenuptial pedicure! Keep your makeup to a minimum, give your cheeks and lips a natural glow with a rosy cheek and lip tint, and delicately define your eyes with a few coats of mascara (waterproof, of course!).

# 10

# Find Your Celebrity Match

## And shine a spotlight on your inner star

Who's Your Supermodel Soul Mate?

Who's Your Sex Symbol Twin?

Which *Sex and the City* Gal Are You?

Who's Your Inner Superhero?

Who's Your Leading Man?

# Who's Your Supermodel Soul Mate?

You've heard all about finding your soul mate when it comes to love and passion. What about your supermodel soul mate? Take this test and find out which leggy bombshell you're most like—and what that says about you.

**1** If you were one of these candies, which would you be?

____ **a.** A Pixie Stick

____ **b.** A Bit-O-Honey

____ **c.** An Atomic FireBall

____ **d.** A Tootsie Roll

**2** Which of these activities is your favorite form of exercise?

____ **a.** Dancing

____ **b.** Yoga

____ **c.** Pilates

____ **d.** Skiing

**3** If you were an animal, you'd probably be

____ **a.** A cute, big-eyed bunny

____ **b.** A graceful, elegant deer

____ **c.** A sleek panther

____ **d.** A cuddly puppy

**4** What's your philosophy when it comes to makeup?

____ **a.** You love to experiment with new colors and looks—after all, makeup should be fun.

____ **b.** Less is more—with mascara and a good lip balm you're happy.

____ **c.** Makeup is a big part of your look, so it's important that you wear the very latest look from the runways.

____ **d.** You have a basic look that you've stuck with for years—who has time to experiment?

**5** What's your morning drink of choice?

____ **a.** Morning? You don't get up before noon!

____ **b.** Herbal tea

____ **c.** A non-fat latte

____ **d.** A big glass of fresh juice

**6** You finally get a reservation at the swanky new bistro in town. Once you get there, you realize they've given away your table. What do you do?

____ **a.** Shrug it off and go have a great time at the bar while you wait for another table.

____ **b.** Take it as a sign that your dining at this restaurant wasn't meant to be and have a great meal at a smaller, less "fabulous" place down the street.

____ **c.** Throw some major attitude until the *maître d'* buckles and gives you another person's table.

____ **d.** Happily go have dinner somewhere else. Who wants to eat at a place that's so pretentious anyway?

**7** In your opinion, which decade was the best? The

____ **a.** '60s

____ **b.** '00s

____ **c.** '90s

____ **d.** '80s

**8** If you were to choose one designer to dress you for a year, who would it be?

____ **a.** Betsey Johnson

____ **b.** Calvin Klein

____ **c.** Donatella Versace

____ **d.** Ralph Lauren

**9** When it comes to shopping for makeup, what's your weakness?

____ **a.** Anything with shimmer, sparkle, or glitter

____ **b.** Skin care

____ **c.** Great lipstick in cool packaging

____ **d.** Free gifts with purchase

## Scoring

Add up the number of As, Bs, Cs, and Ds you chose. Find the category in which you had the most responses to determine your supermodel soul mate.

(Mostly As)
### Twiggy's Soul Mate

Throw on some false lashes and zip up those go-go boots—you share the same free spirit as this queen of mod style! Your fun-loving lifestyle and fearless fashion sense make Twiggy your style soul mate. Twiggy, the first true supermodel, created a totally unique look that's still being imitated today.

Her big eyes, accentuated by lots and *lots* of liner, and her cool, cropped hairstyle made her the model of the moment—for all of the 1960s!

(Mostly Bs)
## Christy's Soul Mate

Your strong belief that beauty comes as much from within as without is a philosophy shared by Christy Turlington. This sweet and subdued supermodel shares your love of classic beauty, opting for chic, casual clothing and cosmetics made from natural ingredients. Her love of all things serene and simple prompted her to create her own line of Ayurvedic skin care and original yoga clothes. So take a tip from your very centered Supermodel soul mate and get out there and do something positive for yourself and others!

(Mostly Cs)
## Naomi's Soul Mate

Your fierce, ever-changing fashion sense and total love of luxury is a perfect match with this *ubermodel* of the '90s. Much like Naomi Campbell, you know what you want and you're not afraid to go get it. In the same way that her extraordinary rise to fame broke all the rules of modeling, you too find a way to overcome obstacles and make any situation work for you. You always know the hottest makeup looks and you're always turning heads by sporting the very latest cut. So go ahead and splurge on that expensive tube of lipstick or that designer bag, because like Naomi, you're worth it!

(Mostly Ds)
## Christie's Soul Mate

As American as apple pie, you share the same wholesome beauty and love of the outdoors as this '80s icon. Like Christie Brinkley, you exude the same girl-next-door charm and appeal that made her one of the most photographed women of her decade. Your sporty style and naturally great hair and skin paired with your easy, outgoing personality make you the life of the party and the person everyone would love to have as a best friend!

# Who's Your Sex Symbol Twin?

Every woman has some sex symbol qualities, whether they're on display or kept hidden. Take this tempting test and find out what type of seductress *you* are—and which hot celebrity you mimic most!

**1** **If you were a men's magazine, you would be**

_____ **a.** *Esquire*

_____ **b.** *Maxim*

_____ **c.** *GQ*

_____ **d.** *Playboy*

**2** **When it's time for bed, what do usually you slip into?**

_____ **a.** Nothing at all

_____ **b.** A baby-doll nightie

_____ **c.** A tank top and pajama bottoms

_____ **d.** Sheer, sexy lingerie

**3** **Your dream date shows up at your door with a gift. Which of these surprises would make you go weak in the knees?**

_____ **a.** A bouquet of red roses

_____ **b.** An adorable stuffed animal

_____ **c.** A DVD of your favorite movie

_____ **d.** Handcuffs

**4** **When you want to set the mood, which of these artists' CDs do you reach for?**

_____ **a.** Frank Sinatra

_____ **b.** Alicia Keys

_____ **c.** Alanis Morissette

_____ **d.** Ozzy Osbourne

**5** **Beauty is more than skin deep, but speaking on a purely surface level, what do you feel is your best feature?**

_____ **a.** Your bedroom eyes

_____ **b.** Your toned midriff

_____ **c.** Your great hair

_____ **d.** Your sexy curves

**6** **You feel most sexy when you're**

_____ **a.** Soaking in a bubble bath

_____ **b.** Dancing all night at the hottest club

_____ **c.** Being active or eating good-for-you food

_____ **d.** Sunbathing in the nude

**7** Your dream bedroom would definitely have

____ **a.** Silk sheets

____ **b.** An amazing sound system

____ **c.** Candles everywhere

____ **d.** A mirror over the bed

**8** What's your idea of the ultimate vacation?

____ **a.** Losing yourself in Paris

____ **b.** Partying on the Vegas Strip

____ **c.** Exploring villages in Thailand

____ **d.** Soaking up the sun in Hawaii

**9** Most of your beauty budget goes toward

____ **a.** Expensive perfumes

____ **b.** The latest makeup colors

____ **c.** High-quality skin care

____ **d.** Tanning

# Scoring

Add up the number of As, Bs, Cs, and Ds you chose. Find the category in which you had the most responses to determine your sex symbol twin—and what that reveals about your powers of seduction.

(Mostly As)

## Marilyn Monroe

The ultimate sex symbol, Marilyn Monroe had the ability to reduce any man to a quivering mound of Jell-O. Like your sex symbol sister, you know how to work a breathy whisper and a knowing glance. Not one to blindly follow the latest beauty trends, you stick with the classics—full red lips, sleekly lined eyes, and strategically placed perfume are all you need to turn heads. When it comes to fashion, you aren't one to bare it all. You pass on the micro-mini and tube top, opting instead for an off-the-shoulder cocktail dress or a snugly fitted sweater. It must be difficult to be such a timeless temptress, what with all those guys stumbling over themselves to open your door. Just remember to leave a few standing for the rest of the female population!

(Mostly Bs)

## Beyoncé Knowles

Like this princess of pop R&B, your sexy style is off the charts. With a tummy that can stop traffic and a star-powered smile, Beyoncé has all eyes on her. Boys want to date her, girls want to be her. You share her "bootylicious" outlook on life and love, and never shy away from embracing the latest trends. When it comes to makeup, you opt to sparkle like the star you are. Your eyes shine with a shimmer eye shadow and glitter eyeliner, your cheeks glow with a little bronzer, and your lips gleam with a fresh pink gloss. As for fashion, you're a firm believer in "less is more." You were born to wear baby Ts and painted-on, low-slung jeans. With the air of a good girl gone glam, you and Ms. Knowles will always steal the show.

(Mostly Cs)

## Jennifer Aniston

Who said smart and sexy don't go hand in hand? Like Jennifer Aniston, you're a woman who knows what she wants. There will be no damsel-in-distress act for you; it's your independence that really drives men wild. A bit of a tomboy at heart, your great body comes from doing push-ups, not wearing a push-up bra. When it comes to beauty, you like to keep it simple, wearing just mascara, a cream blush, and a sheer lipstick in a warm, neutral tone. But more than makeup, you have a natural glow

that comes from eating well and lots of exercise. As for clothes, you love modern designs that show off the figure you've worked so hard to get. A sleek, asymmetrical top or simple strapless dress is all you need to leave men breathless.

(Mostly Ds)

## Pamela Anderson

Watch out, dangerous curves ahead! Supersexy Pamela Anderson is your sultry soul sister. With a figure even Barbie would envy, Pamela is a sex symbol to the 10th power. You both believe in the "if you've got it, flaunt it" philosophy, and like to keep clothing to a minimum. Your closet wouldn't be complete without a few micro-minis, teeny tank tops, and, of course, lots and lots of sexy, strappy sandals. When it comes to makeup, the eyes have it. You opt for smoky shadow and liner followed by a few coats of lengthening mascara. You highlight your tan with a little bronzer and give your lips a sleek sheen with a pale pink gloss. With a sexy style like yours, you're always sure to turn a few heads.

# Which *Sex and the City* Gal Are You?

While you may not be having quite as much sex, chances are you have more in common with the women of the HBO program *Sex and the City* than you realize. Take this quiz to discover which character you resemble most—and what that says about your friends, your career, and your romantic future.

**1** You've been checking a guy out for months, and you're totally smitten. He's the perfect physical specimen and your eye contact has been hot. When you finally get up the nerve to talk to him, he says something both ignorant and gross. You

____ **a.** Figure, hey, he's still cute. He'd at least be good for a fling.

____ **b.** Decide not to waste another breath on him. You just turn and walk away.

____ **c.** Are instantly turned off and look at him like he's crazy. You call your friends and tell them all about it.

____ **d.** Give him a chance to make good. Maybe he's having a bad day.

**2** What's your attitude toward supermodels?

____ **a.** As long as they're confident, powerful, and brazen on the catwalk, you think they're the cat's meow.

____ **b.** As modeling is one of the only professions in which women are paid more than men, you say good for them!

____ **c.** They fascinate you (okay, you're a little jealous), but deep down you know they're totally unrealistic examples of the female species who only make life harder for real women everywhere.

____ **d.** You feel sorry for them because people judge them on their looks and not what's on the inside.

**3** When it comes to sex, you prefer

____ **a.** Wham-bam-thank-you-ma'am quickies

____ **b.** Long, slow, and sensuous lovemaking

____ **c.** A passionate connection and perhaps some playful talk

____ **d.** Candles, music, and verbal declarations of love

**4** **What do the men you date most appreciate about you?**

____ **a.** Your independent spirit and active social life

____ **b.** Your self-confident attitude and devotion to your career

____ **c.** Your quirky style and curious nature

____ **d.** Your traditional values and feminine charms

**5** **A perfect date for you would be**

____ **a.** Dancing most of the night away at the hottest club, then checking in at a four-star hotel

____ **b.** Dinner at a sophisticated restaurant and some good, solid, grown-up conversation

____ **c.** An elegant rooftop party under the stars, full of laughs and sexy teasing

____ **d.** A gourmet picnic in a quiet park, with your date reading to you from a book of poems

**6** **The book you would be most likely to have on your bedside table is**

____ **a.** *Madonna: An Intimate Biography*

____ **b.** *Sandra Day O'Connor: Justice for All (Women of Our Time)*

____ **c.** *Grace: Thirty Years of Fashion at Vogue*

____ **d.** *America's Queen: A Life of Jacqueline Kennedy Onassis*

**7** **The *Sex and the City* gals talk about "having sex like a man." What does that mean to you?**

____ **a.** To call all the shots and be fully satisfied

____ **b.** To feel powerful and not at all vulnerable

____ **c.** To stop thinking and analyzing the situation and just do it

____ **d.** To stop letting your emotions get in the way of your pleasure

**8** **If a guy you've just started dating starts referring to you two as "we," you**

____ **a.** Get annoyed and tell him that you are just you, not part of some vague, presumptuous and premature pronoun

____ **b.** Wonder if he's got the guts to back up that statement with a real commitment

____ **c.** Tease him by saying something like, "Oh, so we're now the royal we?" but secretly find it endearing

____ **d.** Think, "Oh my gosh, he's the one!"

**9** When men whistle at you on the street, you

____ **a.** Smile

____ **b.** Tell them to shove it

____ **c.** Whistle back as a joke

____ **d.** Ignore them

**10** When you and your female friends plan a girls' night out, your job is to

____ **a.** Get a table at the hottest place in town

____ **b.** Tell everyone what she owes when the bill arrives

____ **c.** Keep things lively with your wicked sense of humor

____ **d.** Lend an ear to anyone who needs it

# Scoring

Add up the number of As, Bs, Cs, and Ds you chose. Find the category in which you had the most responses to determine which *Sex and the City* gal you resemble most—and what that says about your friends, your career, and your romantic future. Also check out the other characters you resemble, based on your responses.

(Mostly As)
## Sexy Samantha

You identify with Samantha's bold and liberated qualities. You're strong-willed, larger than life, and you believe in going after what you want—and you usually get it, at work and at play. While your self-confident style is admirable, you have to be careful not to go too far with your self-satisfying ways—or you risk being perceived as selfish and even thoughtless. You have a tendency to get so caught up in craving immediate gratification and excitement that you overlook other people's needs and feelings. Your fashion style most likely reflects your personality: sleek, low-cut, revealing just a bit more than might be considered acceptable. Beware that you're not coming on too strong: You could scare potential suitors off with too much drama. You'll be better off showing less skin and showing off more of your other assets, such as your creativity, leadership skills, and generosity.

(Mostly Bs)
## Shrewd Miranda

You identify with Miranda and her cynical yet sensible ways. Just as she has a tough time deciding whether or not to give in to the affections of men, you don't give your heart up to just anyone. You're cautious in love and seek stability and status in a mate over nearly anything else. Your friends and colleagues admire your steady, realistic attitude, and count on you to bring order out of chaos. Others may not realize that you're secretly incredibly sensual—there's fire beneath those smart business suits. The truth is that you yearn for intimacy but are hesitant to give up your material needs, your career ambitions, and your responsibilities for a passionate moment that might not turn out the way you'd hope. While it's easy to understand why you avoid being hurt in love, you have to take some chances to satisfy the side of you that craves—and deserves—love.

(Mostly Cs)
## Quirky Carrie

Your answers peg you as a Carrie-type—curious and perceptive, and not satisfied with the superficial. While you show some confidence in certain areas of your life, you're often plagued by indecision and try to avoid life's tough issues—especially when it comes to love. While you would be utterly bored by just a pretty face or hot body, you don't mind looking and flirting! You're more turned on, however, by an equally smart and funny mate, someone who challenges your mind and makes you laugh. Plus you love to talk, so you need a good listener. Does such a man exist? You're not sure, but you'll keep looking until you find him. In the meantime, you're certain to be surrounded by friends and admirers, who love your quirky charm, forward fashion sense, intelligence, and wit.

(Mostly Ds)
## Sweet Charlotte

A romantic at heart, you chose the answers that demure Charlotte would have chosen. Intuitive, profound, and sometimes naïve, you're a mother, a mystery, and a poet all in one. You may seem innocent and interested only in seeking the good in people, but you hide yearnings for intimacy, attachment, and ideal love. You're seeking a knight in shining armor, a soul mate who will complete you and tether you to the earth when you get carried away with your fantasies. Be careful not to be so wide-eyed and trusting that you get taken in by some cunning wolf in sheep's clothing. Your super-sensitive ways can be a positive and a negative: You tend to soak up the moods of others, which makes you a highly compassionate friend, but also leaves you vulnerable and overexposed to other people's problems. Likewise, you can be a bit too thin-skinned, and you may want to work on building a better sense of self-empowerment and control. Look to your friends to help you. While they love the fact that they can always count on you to provide a shoulder to cry on, they know you have it in you to be a strong, self-assured woman. And you should know it, too.

# Who's Your Inner Superhero?

Want to bring your superpowers to the surface? Answer these questions to reveal the true identity of your inner superhero— and find out how to boost your female fortitude using fashion and beauty tricks.

**1** You love to wear

____ **a.** Denim

____ **b.** Silk

____ **c.** Suede

____ **d.** Polyester

**2** When you want to a make a big splash at the pool, what do you wear?

____ **a.** A sporty little tankini

____ **b.** A sleek, strapless one-piece

____ **c.** A classic bikini with a sarong wrapped around your waist

____ **d.** A dare-to-bare-it-all thong

**3** What's worse?

____ **a.** A guy with really bad hair

____ **b.** A guy with no job

____ **c.** A guy with a flabby body

____ **d.** A guy without your phone number

**4** You're finally seeing the film you've been anticipating for months. As soon as the movie starts, the people behind you start talking. You

____ **a.** Complain loudly to your friend about their obnoxious behavior, hoping they'll take the hint

____ **b.** Ask them politely to please be quiet

____ **c.** Tell them, not so politely, to shut up

____ **d.** Ignore them, because you're busy making out with your boyfriend

**5** What is your favorite time of day?

____ **a.** Afternoon

____ **b.** Morning

____ **c.** Early evening

____ **d.** Very late at night

**6** Which of these movie titles best describes your love life?

____ **a.** *Night of the Living Dead*

____ **b.** *An Affair to Remember*

____ **c.** *The Jungle Book*

____ **d.** *Some Like It Hot*

**7** If you had to pick one of these perfumes as your signature scent, which would it be?

____ **a.** Calvin Klein's Obsession

____ **b.** Chanel No. 5

____ **c.** Opium by Yves Saint Laurent

____ **d.** Gucci Envy

**8** If you were a shoe, which of these would you be?

____ **a.** Funky cross trainer

____ **b.** Classic stiletto

____ **c.** Comfy sandal

____ **d.** Black, high-heeled leather boot

**9** Which of these is your guilty pleasure?

____ **a.** Watching bad TV shows

____ **b.** Reading tabloids

____ **c.** Eating junk food

____ **d.** Smoking

# Scoring

Add up the number of As, Bs, Cs, and Ds you chose. Find the category in which you had the most responses to determine the true identity of your inner super-hero.

(Mostly As)
## Buffy the Vampire Slayer

Looks can be deceiving. On the outside, you may appear to be the all-American girl, but once the sun goes down—watch out! You've got a wild side that won't be denied. Because doing battle with the creatures of the night can really take it out of a girl, you choose to keep your look simple and chic. You love casual clothes with a funky edge, which works for you, because seeing you in a sexy little tank top and a pair of hipster jeans can drive a stake through any guy's heart! When it comes to beauty, late hours and lots of action call for simple makeup that lasts. For you, waterproof mascara, a little bronzer, and long-wearing lipstick keep you looking great well into the wee hours of the night.

(Mostly Bs)

# Wonder Woman

Proving that being a super heroine doesn't mean sacrificing style, you're able to bowl over the bad guys on looks alone. It takes a fierce fashion sense to have enough vision to skip the cape and opt for a crime-fighting corset. And talk about accessorizing! Who needs a shield when two gold bracelets will do the trick? Because you're not one to be swayed from your true course, you like to stick to the classics. When it comes to makeup, a simple red lipstick, a little powder, and a subtle shadow are the mainstays of your beauty arsenal. And for those days when you're not on duty, your alter ego prefers a simple black dress, pearls, and your signature scent, or a pair of tailored trousers and a crisp white blouse. Your cool, classic style will always make you a hero to women everywhere.

(Mostly Cs)

# Xena, Warrior Princess

You may be a princess, but you're anything but pampered! Being a bit of a tomboy, you prefer keeping your fashion statement to a minimum. Your beauty lies in your strength and courage. You love the durability and edginess of leather and the earthiness of linen and raw silk. When it comes to beauty, the last thing you want is to be burdened with a lot of products. A good moisturizer, a little mascara, and a lip balm (with sunscreen, of course) are all the products a primitive princess like you needs.

(Mostly Ds)

# Catwoman

You're the *purrrfect* blend of naughty and nice. Never afraid to use your feminine wiles to get what you want, you leave men chasing their tails. Sexiness is your super power and you know how to use it. Your feline fashion sense draws you to the luxurious: Slinky silk dresses, an amazing collection of sexy high-heeled shoes, and lots and lots of lingerie are curled up in your closet. As for makeup, you create drama with lots of liquid liner and a lengthening mascara—after all, your eyes are the focal point under that mask. You polish off your look with a little foundation, a clear high-shine lip gloss, and, of course, a few coats of scandalous scarlet polish on your claws!

# Who's Your Leading Man?

Who hasn't fantasized about Hollywood's hottest men—Brad Pitt, Tom Cruise, Antonio Banderas? But have you ever wondered which sexy actors would be perfect for *you*? Here's your chance to find out! This astrological quiz, based on the planetary personalities of your favorite leading men, will reveal which celebrities are your best matches for love—plus which planetary personality to look for in men who don't grace the silver screen.

**1** **Which actress would you most like to invite to your weekly brunch with the girls?**

___ **a.** Cameron Diaz

___ **b.** Gwyneth Paltrow

___ **c.** Kate Winslet

___ **d.** Angelina Jolie

**2** **Where's the *last* place you would go to meet a man?**

___ **a.** A poetry reading

___ **b.** A bowling alley

___ **c.** A house of worship

___ **d.** A rowdy country-western bar

**3** **You're in the men's fragrance area of a department store. Which scents entice you the most?**

___ **a.** Subtle scents that remind you of scenes from childhood: your grandmother's house, your mother's perfume, or freshly cut grass

___ **b.** Spicy scents with notes of vanilla and musk

___ **c.** Floral scents with hints of rose, lilac, and jasmine

___ **d.** Clean, unisex scents that are light and refreshing

**4** **You're sick of the white walls in your bedroom. Which color do you choose to repaint them?**

___ **a.** Black

___ **b.** Pale blue

___ **c.** Apple green

___ **d.** Brick red

**5** **What's your favorite type of guilty-pleasure TV show?**

____ **a.** Trashy talk shows where guests tend to throw chairs

____ **b.** The newest reality TV series

____ **c.** Nature documentaries on PBS or the Discovery Channel

____ **d.** Reruns of your favorite sitcoms from high school

**6** **You've secretly fantasized about dating a**

____ **a.** Sexy professor

____ **b.** Buff carpenter

____ **c.** Male model

____ **d.** Starving artist

**7** **As a child, what were you most likely to get punished for doing?**

____ **a.** Sulking and pouting when you didn't get your way

____ **b.** Teasing and terrorizing the neighborhood boys

____ **c.** Jumping off the top of the jungle gym or swing set

____ **d.** Talking back to your teachers or parents

**8** **Which of these guys would you have invited to your high-school prom?**

____ **a.** The rebel that your parents warned you about

____ **b.** The charming foreign-exchange student

____ **c.** The moody lead singer of a garage band

____ **d.** The class party boy

**9** **If your sister or best friend were setting you up on a blind date, she would be most likely to set you up with a guy who reminded her of**

____ **a.** Bono

____ **b.** Tiger Woods

____ **c.** Ricky Martin

____ **d.** Derek Jeter

**⑩ What would be the ultimate deal-breaker on a first date?**

____ **a.** He says he's too nervous to try sushi, never questions his mother, and doesn't like to travel more than an hour from home.

____ **b.** When asked about his favorite book, he mumbles something about *Sports Illustrated.*

____ **c.** When the waiter isn't looking, he put a piece of his hair into his pasta and loudly complains until he's assured that your dinners will be free of charge.

____ **d.** He invites you to a sports bar, professional wrestling match, or heavy-metal concert.

**⑪ If you were a heroine in a movie, what role would you play?**

____ **a.** The clever ingenue in a historical or costume drama

____ **b.** The adorable girl-next-door in a light romantic comedy

____ **c.** The feisty, butt-kicking crime solver in an electrifying action movie

____ **d.** The alluring detective who solves the crime in a thought-provoking thriller

**⑫ You're in a park full of attractive men. Which one holds your attention?**

____ **a.** The athletic guy who is leading his touch football team to victory

____ **b.** The gorgeous man who is sunning his perfectly toned chest and stomach

____ **c.** The intriguing man who is decisively defeating his opponent at Scrabble

____ **d.** The handsome guy who is patiently coaching Little League

**⑬ If you could live anywhere, you would choose to reside in a**

____ **a.** Brownstone in Boston

____ **b.** Loft in New York City

____ **c.** Guest house in Beverly Hills

____ **d.** Beach house in Miami

## Scoring

Give yourself the numerical value that matches each of your answers. Then add all 13 scores together and use your total score to find your result category.

1. a – 2  b – 3  c – 4  d – 1
2. a – 1  b – 3  c – 2  d – 4
3. a – 4  b – 1  c – 2  d – 3
4. a – 4  b – 3  c – 2  d – 1

5. a – 1  b – 2  c – 3  d – 4
6. a – 3  b – 1  c – 2  d – 4
7. a – 4  b – 2  c – 1  d – 3
8. a – 1  b – 3  c – 4  d – 2
9. a – 4  b – 3  c – 2  d – 1
10. a – 1  b – 3  c – 2  d – 4
11. a – 4  b – 2  c – 1  d – 3
12. a – 1  b – 2  c – 3  d – 4
13. a – 4  b – 3  c – 2  d – 1

(43–52 points)

## Brooding Moon

You're attracted to sensitive, intense men who are influenced by the emotional, ever-changing Moon. Actors such as Tobey Maguire, Johnny Depp, Josh Hartnett, and Ethan Hawke would make perfect leading men for you because they care deeply about their craft. Popular actors who live life like it's a fraternity party do nothing for you; you're more interested in a star's depth and artistic soul. Your leading man needs to be in touch with his feelings—it makes his performance that much more genuine, plus there's something incredibly sexy about a man who isn't afraid to share his vulnerable side. His heartfelt musings are sure to make you swoon. A Moon Man can be moody and temperamental, so give him a little room to brood when he's feeling misunderstood by the cold, cruel world.

(33–42 points)

## Quick-Witted Mercury

Your leading man needs to be clever and smart as a whip. This type of guy has a personality ruled by Mercury, the planet of communication and mental abilities. Actors such as Matthew Broderick, John Cusack, Edward Norton, and Ben Stiller are sharp, funny, and quirky enough to hold their own with you. You're more attracted to actors who come across as intelligent and articulate than ones who get the most fashion spreads in magazines. By contributing his trademark wit and wisdom to his roles, the Mercury-influenced actor adds substance and dimension to his performances. And, let's face it, what could be hotter than an eloquent declaration of love or the ability to quote Shakespeare, Keats, or Frost? Still, the Mercury Man is always chasing the next big idea or role, so you'll need to be creative and resourceful to hold his attention.

(23–32 points)

## Teasing Venus

You're a sucker for a pretty face and a smooth line, so it's not surprising that you're drawn to drop-dead-gorgeous charmers such as George Clooney, Tom Cruise, Ben Affleck, and Brad Pitt. These flirtatious, fun-loving guys embody all that Venus represents: beauty, indulgence, and the eternal search for pleasure. These Venus-influenced actors certainly know how to have a good time, and they defuse tense moments on the set with lighthearted attitude and practical jokes. With their sexy confidence, knack for style, and ability to wrangle reservations at the hottest restaurant, what's not to love about these luscious leading men? Men who are influenced by Venus love the spotlight, however, and tend to resent it when someone steals their thunder. Keeping your Venus Man from getting too big for his britches could become a full-time job!

(13–22 points)
## Masculine Mars

Admit it: You've got a thing for manly men. Actors such as Russell Crowe, Antonio Banderas, and Mel Gibson have probably played starring roles in your fantasies. These passionate, aggressive men are influenced by masculine Mars, which, not surprisingly, is the planet of passion, sexuality, and force. These strong, courageous men possess an adventurous spirit, steely determination, and a commanding sense of power—not a bad mix, especially if you throw in the "bad boy" attitude and bulging biceps. This type of leading man is likely to sweep you off your feet—literally—and bring out your untamed, sensual side. On the flip side, the bold Mars Man is extremely competitive, and his need to win at all costs can lead to all sorts of trouble. Prepare for a bumpy, yet thrilling, ride!

# About the Editor

Eileen Livers, vice president of editorial programming at iVillage, has been developing quizzes for 15 years. Before beginning her iVillage career, she worked as a magazine editor and freelance writer.

# About iVillage

Based in New York City, iVillage Inc. was founded in 1995 with the mission of "humanizing cyberspace." In the early years of the Internet, there were few places for women to find solutions and discuss their problems, needs, and interests. By creating a clean, well-lit space, iVillage carved out a unique place where women could gather and find information and support on a wide range of topics relevant to their lives.

Today, iVillage is a leading women's media company and the number one source for women's information online, providing practical solutions and everyday support for women. iVillage includes iVillage.com, Women.com, Business Women's Network, Lamaze Publishing, The Newborn Channel, iVillage Solutions, Promotions.com, and Astrology.com. The backbone of iVillage is the network of Community Leaders who host thousands of message boards where women exchange practical solutions and support on a daily basis.

iVillage.com's content areas include Astrology, Babies, Beauty, Diet & Fitness, Entertainment, Food, Health, Home & Garden, Lamaze, Money, Parenting, Pets, Pregnancy, Relationships, Shopping, and Work.